SpringerBriefs in Computer Science

For further volumes:
http://www.springer.com/series/10028

Bryan Parno • Jonathan M. McCune • Adrian Perrig

Bootstrapping Trust
in Modern Computers

 Springer

Bryan Parno
Microsoft Research
Redmond, WA
USA
parno@microsoft.com

Jonathan M. McCune
CyLab
Carnegie Mellon University
Pittsburgh, PA
USA
jonmccune@cmu.edu

Adrian Perrig
CyLab
Carnegie Mellon University
Pittsburgh, PA
USA
adrian@ece.cmu.edu

ISSN 2191-5768   e-ISSN 2191-5776
ISBN 978-1-4614-1459-9   e-ISBN 978-1-4614-1460-5
DOI 10.1007/978-1-4614-1460-5
Springer New York Dordrecht Heidelberg London

Library of Congress Control Number: 2011936127

Printed on acid-free paper

Springer is part of Springer Science+Business Media (www.springer.com)

For Diana, Kathleen, and Andrea

Acknowledgements

In May of 2010, we presented a paper entitled *Bootstrapping trust in commodity computers* at the IEEE Symposium on Security and Privacy [152]. There, we were pleased to hear from a number of people that our review paper had taught them a great deal about the area as a whole, or that they planned to distribute it to their students. Their gracious comments inspired us to expand our review into the form you see here. We hope that it will be of service to the security and privacy community.

The authors are especially grateful to our collaborators, Virgil Gligor, Mike Reiter, Arvind Seshadri, Leendert van Doorn, and Amit Vasudevan, whose insights and enthusiasm greatly enriched our work. The authors are also grateful to David Challener, Ron Perez, Reiner Sailer, and Josh Schiffman for their insightful comments, which greatly improved the present work.

This research was supported in part by CyLab at Carnegie Mellon under grants DAAD19-02-1-0389, MURI W 911 NF 0710287, and W911NF-09-1-0273 from the Army Research Office, and grants CNS-0831440 and CCF-0424422 from the National Science Foundation. The views and conclusions contained here are those of the authors and should not be interpreted as necessarily representing the official policies or endorsements, either express or implied, of ARO, CMU, CyLab, Microsoft, NSF, or the U.S. Government or any of its agencies.

Contents

Acronyms

AES	Advanced Encryption Standard
AIK	Attestation Identity Key
AMT	Active Management Technology
API	Application Programming Interface
BBRAM	Battery-Backed RAM
BGP	Border Gateway Protocol
BIND	Binding Instructions aNd Data
BIOS	Basic Input/Output System
CA	Certificate Authority
CFI	Control-Flow Integrity
CLR	Common Language Runtime
CRTM	Core Root of Trust for Measurement
DAA	Direct Anonymous Attestation
DDoS	Distributed Denial-of-Service
DEV	Device Exclusion Vector
DMA	Direct Memory Access
DRAM	Dynamic RAM
DRM	Digital Rights Management
DRTM	Dynamic Root of Trust for Measurement
EK	Endorsement Key
FPGA	Fully-Programmable Gate Array
GPIO	General-Purpose Input/Output
IMA	Integrity Measurement Architecture
IPMI	Intelligent Platform Management Interface
ISP	Internet Service Provider
LED	Light-Emitting Diode
LPC	Low-Pin Count
LS^2	Logic of Secure Systems
LT	LaGrande Technology
MAC	Mandatory Access Control
MLE	Measured Launched Environment
MLTM	Mobile Local-owner Trusted Module
MPT	Memory Protection Table
MPWG	Mobile Phone Working Group

MRTM	Mobile Remote-owner Trusted Module
MTM	Mobile Trusted Module
NAT	Network Address Translation
NGSCB	Next-Generation Secure Computing Base
NTP	Network Time Protocol
NVRAM	Non-Volatile RAM
OAEP	Optimal Asymmetric Encryption Padding
OIAP	Object Independent Authorization Protocol
OS	Operation System
OSLO	Open Secure LOader
PC	Personal Computer
PCI	Peripheral Component Interconnect
PCI-X	PCI Express
PCR	Platform Configuration Register
PIN	Personal Identification Number
PKCS	Public-Key Cryptography Standards
PKI	Public-Key Infrastructure
PRIMA	Policy-Reduced Integrity Measurement Architecture
PUF	Physical Unclonable Function
PXE	Preboot eXecution Environment
RAM	Random-Access Memory
ReDAS	Remote Dynamic Attestation System
ROM	Read-Only Memory
ROTI	Root of Trust Installation
SELinux	Security-Enhanced Linux
SIM	Subscriber Identity Module
SLB	Secure Loader Block
SMI	System-Management Interrupt
SMM	System-Management Mode
SMX	Safer-Mode Extensions
SP	Secret Protected
SSH	Secure Shell
SSL	Secure Socket Layer
SVM	Secure Virtual Machine
TCB	Trusted Computing Base
TCPA	Trusted Computing Platform Alliance
TCG	Trusted Computing Group
TNC	Trusted Network Connect
TOCTOU	Time Of Check, Time Of Use
TOFU	Trust On First Use
TPM	Trusted Platform Module
TSS	TCG Software Stack
TVD	Trusted Virtual Domain
TVEM	Trusted Virtual Environment Module
TXT	Trusted eXecution Technology

USB	Universal Serial Bus
VM	Virtual Machine
VMM	Virtual Machine Monitor
VT	Virtualization Technology
VT-d	Virtualization Technology for Directed IO
vTPM	virtual Trusted Platform Module
WebALPS	Web Applications with Lots of Privacy and Security
XOM	eXecute-Only Memory
ZTIC	Zurich Trusted Information Channel

Abstract and Keywords

Abstract: Trusting a computer for a security-sensitive task (such as checking email or banking online) requires the user to know something about the computer's state. We examine research on securely capturing a computer's state, and consider the utility of this information both for improving security on the local computer (e.g., to convince the user that her computer is not infected with malware) and for communicating a remote computer's state (e.g., to enable the user to check that a web server will adequately protect her data). Although the recent "Trusted Computing" initiative has drawn both positive and negative attention to this area, we consider the older and broader topic of bootstrapping trust in a computer. We cover issues ranging from the wide collection of secure hardware that can serve as a foundation for trust, to the usability issues that arise when trying to convey computer state information to humans. This approach unifies disparate research efforts and highlights opportunities for additional work that can guide real-world improvements in computer security.

Keywords: Bootstrapping, Trusted Computing, Secure Boot, Trusted Platform Module, Secure Hardware

1 Introduction

Suppose you are presented with two physically identical computers. One is running a highly-certified, formally-proven, time-tested software stack, while the other is running a commodity software stack that provides similar features, but is infested with sophisticated malware. How can you tell which computer is which? How can you decide which computer you should use to check your email, update your medical records, or access your bank account?

While the design and validation of secure software is an interesting study in its own right, we focus this book on a survey of existing techniques for bootstrapping trust in commodity computers, specifically by conveying information about a computer's current execution environment to an interested party. This would, for example, enable a user to verify that her computer is free of malware, or that a remote web server will handle her data responsibly.

To better highlight the research aspects of bootstrapping trust, we organize this book thematically, rather than chronologically. Thus, we examine mechanisms for securely collecting and storing information about the execution environment (Section 2), methods for using that information locally (Section 3), techniques for securely conveying that information to an external party (Section 4), and various ways to convert the resulting information into a meaningful trust decision (Section 5).

Bootstrapping trust requires some foundational *root of trust*, and we review various candidates in Section 6. We then consider how the process of bootstrapping trust can be validated (Section 8) and used in applications (Section 9). Of course, creating trust ultimately involves human users, which creates a host of additional challenges (Section 11). Finally, all of the work we survey has certain fundamental limitations (Section 12).

Much of the research in this area falls under the heading of "Trusted Computing", the most visible aspect of which is the Trusted Platform Module (TPM), which has already been deployed on over 350 million computers [219]. In many ways, this is one of the most significant changes in hardware-supported security in commodity systems since the development of segmentation and process rings *in the 1960s*, and yet it has been met with muted interest in the security research community, perhaps due to its perceived association with Digital Rights Management (DRM) [6]. However, like any other technology, the TPM can be used for either savory or unsavory purposes. One goal of this book is to highlight the many ways in which it can be used to improve user security without restricting user flexibility.

While Trusted Computing is the most visible aspect of this research area, we show that many of the techniques used by Trusted Computing date back to the 1980s [68]. These ideas thus extend beyond Trusted Computing's TPM to the general concept of bootstrapping trust in commodity computers. This fact becomes all the more relevant as cellphones emerge as the next major computing platform (as of 2005, the number of cellphones worldwide was about double the number of personal computers [80, 218]). In fact, many cellphones already incorporate stronger hardware support for security than many desktop computers and use some of the techniques described in this book [9, 13]. Indeed, as CPU transistor counts continue to climb, CPU vendors are increasingly willing to provide hardware support for secure systems (see, for example, Intel and AMD's support for virtualization [3, 93], and Intel's new AES instructions, which provide greater efficiency and resistance to side-channel attacks [81]). Thus, research in this area can truly guide the development of new hardware-supported security features.

Summary

In this book, we endeavor to:

1. Draw attention to the opportunities presented by the spread of commodity hardware support for security;
2. Provide a unified presentation of the reasoning behind and the methods for bootstrapping trust; and
3. Present existing research in a coherent framework, highlighting underexamined areas, and hopefully preventing the reinvention of existing techniques.

While we aim to make this book accessible to those new to the area, we do not intend to provide a comprehensive tutorial on the various technologies; instead, we refer the interested reader to the various references, particularly those highlighted in Section 13, for additional details.

2 What Do We Need to Know?
Techniques for Recording Platform State

In deciding whether to trust a platform, it is desirable to learn about its current state. In this section, we discuss why code identity is a crucial piece of platform state and how to measure it (Section 2.1). We then consider additional dynamic properties that may be of interest, e.g., whether the running code respects information-flow control (Section 2.2). Finally, we argue that establishing code identity is a more fundamental property than establishing any of the other dynamic properties discussed (Section 2.3). Unfortunately, the security offered by many of these techniques is still brittle, as we discuss in Section 12.

2.1 Recording Code Identity

Why Code Identity?

To trust an entity X with her private data (or with a security-sensitive task), Alice must believe that at no point in the future will she have cause to regret having given her data (or entrusted her task) to X. In human interactions, we often form this belief on the basis of identity – if you know someone's identity, you can decide whether to trust them. However, while user identity suffices for some tasks (e.g., authorizing physical access), buggy software and user inexperience makes it difficult for a user to vouch for the code running on their computer. For example, when Alice attempts to connect her laptop to the corporate network, the network can verify (e.g., using a password-based protocol) that Alice is indeed at the laptop. However, *even if* Alice is considered perfectly trustworthy, this *does not* mean that Alice's laptop is free of malware, and hence it may or may not be safe to allow the laptop to connect.

Thus, to form a belief about a computer's future behavior, we need to know more than the identity of its user. One way to predict a computer's behavior is to learn its complete current state. This state will be a function of the computer's hardware configuration, as well as the code it has executed. While hardware configuration might be vouched for via a signed certificate from the computer's manufacturer, software state is more ephemeral, and hence requires us to establish *code identity* before we can make a trust decision.

Of course, the question remains: what constitutes code identity? At present, the state-of-the-art for identifying software is to compute a cryptographic hash over the software's binary, as well as any inputs, libraries, or configuration files used. The resulting hash value is often termed a *measurement*. We discuss some of the difficulties with the interpretation of this type of measurement, as well as approaches to convert such measurements into higher-level properties, in Section 5. Note that in this work, we will often refer to "code", "software", and "binary" interchangeably, relying on context to resolve any ambiguity.

What Code Needs To Be Recorded?

To bootstrap trust in a platform, we must, at the very least, record the identity of the code currently in control of the platform. More subtly, we also need to record the identity of any code that could have affected the security of the currently executing code. For example, code previously in control of the platform might have configured the environment such that the currently running code behaves unexpectedly or maliciously. In the context of the IBM 4758 secure coprocessor [184, 185], Smith analyzes in greater detail which pieces of code can affect the security of a given piece of software [182], examining issues such as previously installed versions of an application that may have accessed the currently installed application's secrets.

Who Performs the Measurements?

The best time to measure a piece of software is before it starts to execute. At this point, it is in a fresh "canonical" form that is likely to be similar across many platforms [68, 127]. Once it starts executing, it will generate local state that may vary across platforms, making it difficult to evaluate the measurement. Thus, if the software currently in control of the platform is S_n, then the logical entity to measure S_n is the software that was previously in control of the platform, i.e., S_{n-1}. In other words, before executing S_n, S_{n-1} must contain code to record a measurement of S_n in its "pristine" state. This logical progression continues recursively, with each software S_i responsible for measuring software S_{i+1} before giving it control of the platform. These measurements document the *chain of trust* [213]; i.e., the party interpreting the measurements must trust each piece of software to have properly measured and recorded subsequently launched pieces of software. Of course, this leads to the question of who (or what) measures the first software (S_1) to execute on the system.

Ultimately, measuring code identity requires a hardware-based *root of trust*. After all, if we simply ask the running code to self-identify, malicious software will lie. As we discuss in Section 6, most research in this area uses secure hardware (e.g., secure coprocessors) for this purpose, but some recent work considers the use of general-purpose CPUs.

Thus, in a *trusted boot* (a technique first introduced by Gasser et al. [68]), a hardware-based root of trust initiates the chain of trust by measuring the initial BIOS code (see Figure 1). The BIOS then measures and executes the bootloader, and the bootloader, in turn, measures and executes the operating system. Note that trusted boot *does not* mean that the software that has booted is necessarily trustworthy, merely that it must be trusted if the platform itself is to be trusted.

This process of temporal measurement collection can be extended to include additional information about less privileged code as well (i.e., code that is not in control of the platform). For example, the OS might record measurements of each application that it executes. On a general-purpose platform, this additional information is crucial to deciding if the platform is currently in a trustworthy state, since

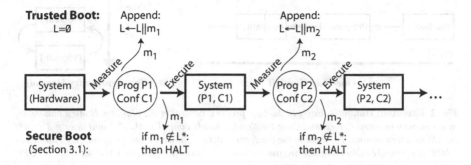

Fig. 1 Trusted Boot vs. Secure Boot. *The state of a computer system changes as programs run with particular configurations. Trusted boot accumulates a list (L) of measurements for each program executed, but it does not perform any enforcement. Secure boot (§3.1) will halt the system if any attempt is made to execute a program that is not on an approved list (L*). Note that both systems must always measure programs before executing them. It is also possible to employ both types of boot simultaneously [68].*

most modern operating systems do not, by themselves, provide enough assurance as to the security of the entire system.

On the other hand, if the software in control of the platform can be trusted to protect itself from, and maintain isolation between, less privileged code, then it may only need to record measurements of less privileged code that performs security-sensitive operations. For example, the Terra project [64] observed that a trusted virtual machine monitor (VMM) can implement a trusted boot model both for itself and its virtual machines (VMs). This approach simplifies measurement, since the measurement of a single VM image can encompass an entire software stack. Furthermore, since a VMM is generally trusted to isolate itself from the VMs (and the VMs from each other), the VMM need only record measurements for the VMs that perform security-relevant actions.

Of course, virtualization can also complicate the use of secure hardware, since each VM may want or need exclusive control of it. The virtual Trusted Platform Module (vTPM) project [20] investigated how a single physical TPM can be multiplexed across multiple VMs, providing each with the illusion that it has dedicated access to a TPM.

IBM researchers also coined the notion of a Trusted Virtual Domain (TVD), which is a management perspective on distributed systems that focuses on service domains instead of point hardware and software solutions [29]. The TVD concept includes the notion of platform integrity stemming from TPM-based measurements, and shows how one might integrate such properties across a larger distributed system. The TVD concept has inspired other researchers to further develop the concept, e.g., [16, 34, 67, 125]. However, a detailed treatment is beyond the scope of the present work, and we refer interested readers to Section 13.

Other researchers have investigated similar directions. For example, Krautheim et al. propose the Trusted Virtual Environment Module (TVEM), which is in one

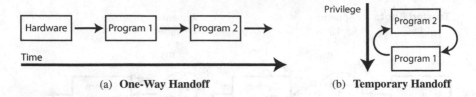

(a) **One-Way Handoff**   (b) **Temporary Handoff**

Fig. 2 Execution Handoffs. *Early in the boot process, control of the platform is often handed off in a one-way manner. For example, the bootloader hands control to the OS and does not expect the OS to return control. For most of the platform's lifetime, however, one program (e.g., the OS or VMM) temporarily allows another program to run (e.g., an application or VM), but relies on CPU privilege mechanisms to eventually return control.*

sense an enhanced vTPM, with more awareness of the semantics of distributed and virtualized applications [110]. Goldman et al. propose logging extensions to vTPMs to support better scalability in the data center [76].

How Can Measurements Be Secured?

Of course, all of these code identity records must be secured; otherwise, malicious code might erase the record of its presence. This can happen in one of two ways (see Figure 2), depending on the way in which control of the platform is handed off.

First, software currently in control of the platform can make a one-way transfer of control, with no intention of returning. For example, during the boot process, the bootloader hands control to the OS, with no intention of resuming execution. In a *handoff attack*, trusted software inadvertently cedes control of the platform to malicious software. For example, if the attacker replaces the standard OS with a malicious OS, the bootloader may inadvertently hand control of the platform to the malicious OS during the boot process. The malicious software, now in control of the entire platform, may then attempt to erase any previously created records.

Second, software currently in control of the platform can make a temporary execution transfer and rely on CPU features like privilege layers to eventually return control. For example, the OS temporarily allows applications to run, or a VMM allows its VMs to run, but both expect to resume execution in the future. In a *privilege escalation attack*, less privileged code may find an exploit in more privileged code, allowing it to access that code's secrets, erase the record of the malicious code's presence, or even create fake records of other software.

Unfortunately, existing literature [64, 68, 164] tends to conflate these two types of attacks, obscuring the relative merits of techniques for securing measurements (see Figure 3). Below, we explore these techniques, certificate chains and hash chains, in more detail. While some research proposes to secure records via a general-purpose, secure append-only log [170], such work makes use of an independent logging server which is not available in many environments.

		Attack Type	
		Privilege Escalation	**Handoff Control to Malcode**
Chain Type	**Hash**	Record latest value in HW	Record latest value in HW
	Cert	Vulnerable!	Prove access to latest key

Fig. 3 Securely Recording Code Measurements. *Techniques for preventing attacks on the measurement record differ based on the method used to secure the record.*

CERTIFICATE CHAINS.

Initial architecture designs for recording code identity measurements employed certificate chains [64, 68]. Before loading a new piece of software, Gasser et al. require the currently running system to generate a certificate for the new software [68]. To do so, the currently running system generates a new keypair for use by the new software and uses its private key to sign a certificate containing the new public key and a measurement of the new software. The system then erases its own secrets and loads the new software, providing the new keypair and certificate as inputs. As a result, a certificate chain connects the keypair held by the currently running software all the way back to the computer's hardware.

More concretely, consider the boot sequence shown in Figure 1. The hardware is assumed to hold the private key SK_H corresponding to a well-known public key PK_H. Before executing Program 1, it generates a fresh keypair $\{PK_1, SK_1\}$, and generates a certificate binding the keypair to the program's measurement, i.e., $\textbf{Sign}_{SK_H}(PK_1||P_1||C_1)$. Program 1, before it executes Program 2, generates a fresh keypair $\{PK_2, SK_2\}$, and generates a certificate for it, i.e., $\textbf{Sign}_{SK_1}(PK_2||P_2||C_2)$. It erases its own private key, SK_1, and then starts executing Program 2, providing as input the new keypair (i.e., $\{PK_2, SK_2\}$), and the current certificate chain, i.e., $\textbf{Sign}_{SK_H}(PK_1||P_1||C_1)$, $\textbf{Sign}_{SK_1}(PK_2||P_2||C_2)$.

Certificate chains prevent handoff attacks, since by the time malicious code is loaded, the keys used to generate the certificate chain have been erased (this is an important point, often omitted in later work [64]). For example, by the time Program 2 executes, SK_1 has been erased (and the hardware will only use SK_H to sign the first piece of software it launches). Thus, the only keypair the malicious code can both use (in the sense of knowing the private key) and produce a certificate chain for, is a keypair ($\{PK_2, SK_2\}$) that is certified with a certificate containing the measurement of the malicious code. Thus, by requiring code to prove knowledge of a certified keypair, a remote entity can ensure that it receives an accurate measurement list.

A certificate chain, however, cannot prevent a privilege escalation attack from subverting the measurements. To maintain the certificate chain, privileged code must keep its private key available; i.e., it cannot delete its key like it did during a one-way handoff. To see this, consider an OS that wishes to extend a certificate chain to cover each application executed. If the OS erases its secret key before handing control to Application 1, then it will not be able to generate a certificate for applications launched later.

Because privileged code must keep its private key in memory, a privilege-escalated attacker can use that key to rewrite the chain. In other words, the attacker can generate a fresh keypair, $\{PK_A, SK_A\}$, and then use the more privileged software's (e.g., the OS's) private key to bind the keypair to a benign program BP's measurement by generating $\mathbf{Sign}_{SK_{OS}}(PK_A||P_{BP}||C_{BP})$. At this point the attacker can arbitrarily rewrite the portion of the platform's chain of trust following the vulnerable software. For example, if the OS is vulnerable, then once the attacker exploits this vulnerability, he can arbitrarily rewrite the list of applications loaded. He may not, however, be able to remove the vulnerable OS from the list, since the OS is typically loaded via a one-way handoff, and hence the bootloader's keys are no longer available.

HASH CHAINS.

Hash chains represent a potentially more efficient method of recording software measurements. A hash chain requires only a constant amount of secure memory to record an arbitrarily long, append-only list of code identities. As long as the current value of the hash chain is stored in secure memory, both privilege escalation and handoff attacks can be prevented. This is the approach adopted by the Trusted Platform Module (TPM) [213]. Several research efforts have applied this approach to the Linux kernel, and developed techniques to improve its efficiency [127, 164].

For a hardware-backed hash chain, the hardware sets aside a protected memory register that is initialized to a known value (e.g., 0) when the computer first boots. On a TPM, these protected memory registers are called Platform Configuration Registers (PCR); current (version 1.2) TPMs are required to support at least 24 PCRs [213]. The software determining a new code module's identity I uses a hardware API to *extend I* into the log. The hardware computes a cryptographic hash over the the identity record and the current value V of the register and updates the register with the output of the hash: $V \leftarrow \texttt{Hash}(V||I)$. The software may keep an additional log of I in untrusted storage to help with the interpretation of the register's value at a future point. As long as $\texttt{Hash}$ is collision-resistant, the register value V guarantees the integrity of the append-only log; i.e., even if malicious software gains control of the platform (via privilege escalation or a control handoff), it cannot erase its identity from the log without rebooting the platform and losing control of the machine.

Of course, without secure storage of the current value of the hash chain, a hash chain cannot protect the integrity of the log, since once malicious code gains control, it can simply replay the earlier extend operations and omit its measurement. There are no secret keys missing that would impede it.

TPM-Based Measurement Example

To make this discussion more concrete, we give an example of a TPM-based trusted boot sequence. This example is highly simplified; IBM's Integrity Measurement

Architecture (IMA) discusses the design and implementation of a much more complete solution for performing measurements [164]. We assume that the BIOS ($\mathscr{B}$), the bootloader ($\mathscr{L}$), and the operating system ($\mathscr{O}$) have all been modified to support measurement collection. In practice, the BIOS and other firmware on many motherboards often does not support such measurements, and hence must be updated before a chain of trust can be established. These legacy issues helped motivate the introduction of a CPU-based operation to create a dynamic root of trust after the platform boot sequence (see Section 5.2).

When the computer first boots, the TPM's PCRs are initialized to a known value (e.g., 0). ROM code then measures (computes a hash) of the BIOS ($\mathscr{B}$) and invokes PCRExtend with a canonical PCR index, e.g., 5:

$$\text{PCRExtend}(5, \mathscr{B})$$

As a result, the TPM computes:

$$PCR_5 \leftarrow H(0 \| \mathscr{B})$$

The ROM code then starts executing the BIOS. The BIOS performs its usual initialization routines and extends a measurement of the bootloader ($\mathscr{L}$) into the TPM. It could choose a different PCR, but we will assume it continues to use PCR_5, so we have:

$$PCR_5 \leftarrow H(\underline{H(0 \| \mathscr{B})} \| \mathscr{L})$$

The underlined value simply represents the previous value of PCR_5. After the PCRExtend operation, the BIOS can launch the bootloader. Similarly, the bootloader will extend a measurement of the OS ($\mathscr{O}$) into the TPM before starting to execute it. Finally, the OS will extend a measurement of the application ($\mathscr{A}$) into the TPM and launch the application. As a result, the value of PCR_5 is :

$$h = H(H(H(\underline{H(0 \| \mathscr{B})} \| \mathscr{L}) \| \mathscr{O}) \| \mathscr{A})$$

Notice that the entire boot sequence is captured in a single hash value. Sections 3–5 discuss how to use and interpret this information.

2.2 Recording Dynamic Properties

While code identity is an important property, it is often insufficient to guarantee security. After all, even though the system may start in a secure state, external inputs may cause it to arrive in an insecure state. Thus, before entrusting a computer with sensitive data, it might be useful to know whether the code has followed its intended control flow (i.e., that it has not been hijacked by an attack), preserved the integrity of its data structures (e.g., the stack is still intact), or maintained some form of information-flow control. We compare the merits of these dynamic properties to those of code identity in Section 2.3. Below, we discuss two approaches, load-time and run-time, to capturing these dynamic properties.

The simplest way to capture dynamic properties is to transform the program itself and then record the identity of the transformed program. For example, the XFI [56] and CFI [1] techniques transform a code binary by inserting inline reference monitors that enforce a variety of properties, such as stack and control-flow integrity. By submitting the transformed binary to the measurement infrastructure described in Section 2.1, we record the fact that a program with the appropriate dynamic property enforcements built-in was loaded and executed. If the transformation is trusted to perform correctly, then we can extrapolate from the code identity that it also has the property enforced by the transformation. Of course, this approach does not protect against attacks that do not tamper with valid control flows [40]. For example, a buffer overflow attack might overwrite the Boolean variable isAdministrator to give the attacker unexpected privileges.

Another approach is to load some piece of code that is trusted to dynamically enforce a given security property on less-privileged code. An early example of this approach is "semantic" attestation [85], in which a language runtime (e.g., the Java or .NET virtual machine) monitors and records information about the programs it runs. For example, it might report dynamic information about the class hierarchy or that the code satisfies a particular security policy. As a concrete example of this approach, Vejda et al. develop language-based trust services for the Java virtual machine [217]. In a similar spirit, the ReDAS system [105] loads a kernel that has been instrumented to check certain application data invariants at each system call. Trust in the kernel and the invariants that it checks can allow an external party to conclude that the applications running on the kernel have certain security-relevant properties. Again, this approach relies on a code identity infrastructure to identify that the trusted monitor was loaded.

Similarly, Baiardi et al. investigate methods for introspection of a target system to dynamically confirm desired behavior at runtime [15]. While virtual-machine based introspection is a known concept, their work shows how to integrate such mechanisms with remote attestation.

2.3 Which Property is Necessary?

As discussed above, there are many code properties that are relevant to security, i.e., things we would like to know about the code on a computer before entrusting it with a security-sensitive task. However, since a general-purpose CPU can devote only a limited amount of real estate to security functionality, we must consider what properties are fundamentally needed (as opposed to merely being more efficient in hardware).

The discussion in Section 2.2 suggests that many dynamic properties can be achieved (in some sense) using code identity. In other words, the identity of the code conveys the dynamic properties one can expect from it or the properties that one can expect it to enforce on other pieces of software. However, the converse does not appear to be true. That is, if a hardware primitive could report, for example, that the currently running code respected its intended control flow, then it is not clear how to use that mechanism to provide code identity. Furthermore, it clearly does not suffice to say anything meaningful about the security-relevant behavior of the code. A malicious program may happily follow its intended control-flow as it conveys the user's data to an attacker. Similar problems appear to affect other potential candidates as well. Knowing that a particular invariant has been maintained, whether it is stack integrity or information-flow control, is not particularly useful without knowing more about the context (that is the code) in which the property is being enforced.

Thus, one can argue that code identity truly is a fundamental property for providing platform assurance, and thus a worthy candidate for hardware support. Of course, this need not preclude additional hardware support for monitoring (or enforcing) dynamic properties.

3 Can We Use Platform Information Locally?

We now discuss how accumulated platform information (Section 2) can benefit a local user. Unfortunately, these measurements cannot be used to directly provide information to local software; i.e., it does not make sense for higher-privileged software to use these measurements to convey information to less-privileged software, since the less-privileged software must already trust the higher-privileged software.

Nonetheless, in this section, we review techniques for using these measurements to convince the user that the platform has booted into a secure state, as well as to provide access control to a protected storage facility, such that secrets will only be available to a specific software configuration in the future. Such techniques tend to focus on preserving the secrecy and integrity of secrets, with less emphasis placed on availability. Indeed, using code identity for access control can make availability guarantees fragile, since a small change to the code (made for malicious or legitimate reasons) may make secret data unavailable.

3.1 Secure Boot

How can a user tell if her computer has booted into a secure state? One approach is to use a technique first described by Gasser et al. [68] and later dubbed "secure boot" [8].

In a computer supporting secure boot, each system component, starting with the computer's boot ROM, compares the measurement of code to be loaded to a list of measurements for authorized software (authorization is typically expressed via a signature from a trusted authority, which requires the authority's public key to be embedded in the computer's firmware) [8, 68]. Secure boot halts the boot process if there is an attempt to load unauthorized code, and thus assures the user that the platform is in an approved state simply by booting successfully.

One of the first systems to actually implement these ideas was AEGIS[1] [8]. With AEGIS, before a piece of software is allowed to execute, its identity is checked against a certificate from the platform's owner. The certificate identifies permitted software. Anything without a certificate will not be executed.

However, a remote party cannot easily determine that a computer has been configured for secure boot. Even if it can make this determination, it only learns that the computer has booted into some authorized state, but it does not learn any information about what specific state it happens to be in. Section 4 discusses the techniques needed to provide more information to a remote party.

---

[1] Two relevant research efforts have used the name AEGIS. One is that of Arbaugh et al. [8] discussed in this section. The other is a design for a secure coprocessor by Suh et al. [201] and is discussed in Section 6.1.

3.2 Storage Access Control Based on Code Identity

Applications often require long-term protection of the secrets that they generate. Practical examples include the keys used for full disk encryption or email signatures, and a list of stored passwords for a web browser. Abstractly, we can provide this protection via an access control mechanism for cryptographic keys, where access policies consist of sets of allowed platform configurations, represented by the measurement lists described in Section 2. Below, we discuss two of the most prominent protected storage solutions: the IBM 4758 cryptographic co-processor and the Trusted Platform Module (TPM).

3.2.1 Tamper-Responding Protected Storage

The IBM 4758 family of cryptographic co-processors provides a rich set of secure storage facilities [50, 99, 184, 185]. First and foremost, it incorporates tamper-responding storage in battery-backed RAM (BBRAM). Additional flash memory is also available, but the contents of flash are always encrypted with keys maintained in BBRAM. The design intention is that any attempt to physically tamper with the device will result in it actively erasing secrets. Cryptographic keys that serve as the root for protected storage can be kept here.

The IBM 4758 enforces storage access restrictions based on the concept of software privilege layers. Layer 0 is read-only firmware. Layer 1 is, by default, the IBM-provided CP/Q++ OS. Layers 2 and 3 are for applications. Each layer can store secrets either in BBRAM or in flash. A hardware ratcheting lock prevents a lower-privilege layer from accessing the state of a higher-privilege layer. Thus, once an application loads at layer 2 or 3, the secrets of layer 1 are unavailable. Extensions to the OS in layer 1 could permit arbitrarily sophisticated protected storage properties; for example, an extension could provide a sealed storage facility (similar to the TPM functionality discussed below) for binding secrets to a particular software configuration. The BBRAM is also ideal for storing secure counters, greatly simplifying defense against state replay attacks.

3.2.2 TPM-Based Sealed Storage

Despite providing much less functionality than a full-blown secure coprocessor, the TPM can also restrict storage access based on platform state. It does so by allowing software on the platform's main CPU to *seal* or *bind* secrets to a set of measurements representing some future platform state (we discuss the differences between these operations below). Both operations (seal and bind) essentially encrypt the secret value provided by the software. The TPM will refuse to perform a decryption, unless the current values in its Platform Configuration Registers (PCRs – see Section 2.1) match those specified during the seal or bind operation.

Full disk encryption is an example of an application that benefits from sealed storage. The disk encryption keys can be sealed to measurements representing the user's operating system. Thus, the disk can only be decrypted if the intended OS kernel has booted. This is the basic design of Microsoft BitLocker, discussed in Section 9. Connecting disk encryption with code identity ensures that even if an attacker modifies the boot sequence to load malware (e.g., via a DVD) or an alternate OS kernel (e.g., an older kernel with known vulnerabilities), that software will be unable to access the disk's contents.

To provide protected storage, both (seal and bind) operations use encryption with 2048-bit asymmetric RSA keys, where the corresponding private keys are internal to the TPM. The RSA keys are generated on the TPM itself, and the private portions are never released in the clear. The TPM also ensures that these keys are only used for encryption operations and never for signing [213]. Because the encryptions use RSA PKCS #1v2.0 OAEP padding, the resulting encryption scheme is IND-CCA secure [61], meaning that any change to the ciphertext will be detected during the decryption process; hence the encryption scheme provides both secrecy and integrity for the underlying plaintext.

Since the TPM has only a limited amount of protected internal storage space, it uses a key hierarchy to protect storage keys. Specifically, the TPM stores only the private portion of its *Storage Root Keypair* in protected storage. It then uses the public portion of the Storage Root Keypair to encrypt the private portion of keys used for seal and bind operations. The computer's software (e.g., the OS or VMM) is then responsible for managing the resulting ciphertext. Before performing a seal/bind operation, the software loads a key into the TPM by presenting it with a ciphertext encrypted by the Storage Root Key. The TPM decrypts the ciphertext to obtain a key, checks its integrity, and then uses it to perform the seal/bind operation. In this way, the TPM supports an arbitrary number of storage keys while using only a constant amount of protected storage.

This approach does mean that software can destroy storage keys (by deleting the corresponding ciphertexts), but this is considered a denial-of-service attack, which the software controlling the platform can always launch in other ways as well, e.g., by powering off the computer, or wiping the hard drive.

In practice, for greater efficiency, applications that wish to protect large amounts of data will typically use freshly generated symmetric keys for encryption and integrity protection of the data, and then use the TPM to protect the symmetric keys.

Sealing Data

Software on a TPM-equipped platform can invoke the TPM's *seal* operation to encrypt a secret value and specify a policy that controls the decryption of the resulting ciphertext. The policy specifies a set of PCR indices and the values those PCRs should hold in order for the secret to be released; note that these values may be different from the current PCR values. In the future, when software wishes to decrypt the ciphertext that resulted from the seal operation, it asks the TPM to *unseal* it. The

TPM decrypts the ciphertext internally; if the current values in the specified PCRs match the values specified in the policy, the TPM releases the plaintext (see below for a concrete example).

The ability to seal data to an arbitrary set of PCR values enables a variety of scenarios, including secure software updates. Suppose a software module P decides to upgrade to a new version P'. Once P has validated the upgrade (e.g., by using the publisher's public key to verify a signature over the binary for P'), P unseals all of its private data and then passes that data to a seal operation, specifying PCR values corresponding to P'. When P' runs, the PCR values will match, and hence the upgraded version of the program will have access to all of the prior version's data.

Because the TPM's seal operation requires the RSA encryption to take place on the TPM, the TPM can also include the *current* values of any specified PCRs (which may be different from the values specified in the decryption policy) in the resulting ciphertext. When the data is later decrypted, the software that performs the unseal operation can ascertain the exact identity of the software that invoked the original seal command. This allows an application that unseals data to determine whether the newly unsealed data should be trusted. This may be useful, for example, during software updates, allowing the new version to check that any data imported via an unseal operation really did come from the previous version of the software.

Because sealing and unsealing require the same TPM to perform the encryption/decryption operations, it would be much more efficient to use a symmetric encryption scheme, such as AES. However, at the time of its design, the TPM was encumbered by export controls that precluded the use of desired algorithms.

Binding Data

In contrast to sealing, encryption using a public binding key need not take place on the TPM. This allows for greater efficiency and flexibility when performing data encryption, but it means that the resulting ciphertext does not include a record of the entity that originally invoked the bind operation. However, because the private key used for *un*binding data can be locked to PCR values, an entity in possession of an authentic public binding key can encrypt data (e.g., a cryptographic challenge such as a nonce) using a binding key, and hence learn something about the software state of the platform that performed the unbind operation.

Employing NVRAM

The TPM also includes a limited amount of nonvolatile RAM (NVRAM) that can be used to perform a function similar to sealed storage. In particular, reading and writing to NVRAM can be restricted based on the contents of the PCRs, so an NVRAM location can be made accessible only to a particular collection of software. Since an NVRAM location can store arbitrary data, the most straightforward approach to "sealing" data is to define an NVRAM location large enough to hold a symmetric key and use the PCR-based restrictions to prevent other software from reading or writing the key. The symmetric key can then be used to encrypt and MAC bulk data.

There are multiple limitations when using NVRAM. First, software that does not match the PCR restrictions on an NVRAM location may still be able to delete the information stored in that location. For example, the TPM owner can both delete and re-establish NVRAM locations. Thus, application developers must be cautious when using this facility. In particular, code reading or writing an NVRAM location should verify that the target location has the expected PCR-based restrictions in place. Second, the v1.2 TPM specification only requires 1,280 bytes of NVRAM, some of which is dedicated to various system features such as storing the TPM's endorsement credential and the launch control policy. Although reading NVRAM is relatively fast (9.8–14.8 ms) compared to other TPM operations, writing is 3–6x slower (33.9–82.4 ms) [151]. Finally, the NVRAM is only expected to tolerate a limited number ($\sim$100,000) of write cycles during its lifetime. Writing to NVRAM once every second would exhaust its write cycles in less than 28 hours.

Replay Issues

Note that the above-mentioned schemes bind cryptographic keys to some representation of software identity (e.g., hashes stored in PCRs). Absent from these primitives is any form of freshness or replay-prevention. The output of a seal or bind operation is ciphertext. Decryption depends on PCR values and an optional 20-byte authorization value. It does not depend on any kind of counter or versioning system. Application developers must take care to account for versioning of important sealed state, as older ciphertext blobs can also be decrypted. An example attack scenario is when a user changes the password to their full disk encryption system. If the current password is maintained in sealed storage, and the old password is leaked, certain classes of adversaries may be able to supply an old ciphertext at boot time and successfully decrypt the disk using the old password. The TPM includes a basic monotonic counter that can be used to provide such replay protection. However, the TPM has no built-in support for combining sealed storage with the monotonic counter. NVRAM may be a better choice than sealed storage for such an application.

To address these shortcomings and simplify development, Parno et al. designed and implemented the Memoir framework [151]. Memoir provides *state continuity*, i.e., integrity, secrecy, and rollback-resistance for the state on which security-sensitive software operates. In particular, it provides rollback resistance without making the system vulnerable to system crashes (unlike, say a solution based on monotonic counters). Memoir achieves these properties by enforcing module determinism, storing a concise summary of the module's request history in trusted storage, and allowing only safe request replays after crashes. Since frequent writes to trusted, non-volatile storage on the TPM is impractical (due to the latency of write operations and the limited number of write cycles supported by the specification), the authors show how to spread the state summary across both volatile and non-volatile trusted storage. The protocols involved were formally proven correct using machine-checked proofs, and the implementation is available.

TPM-Based Sealed Storage Example

Here we continue the example begun in Section 2.1. Recall that we assumed that the BIOS ($\mathscr{B}$), the bootloader ($\mathscr{L}$) and the operating system ($\mathscr{O}$) have all been modified to record the appropriate code identity records in the TPM. If the OS is currently running an application ($\mathscr{A}$), then the value of PCR_5 is :

$$h = H(H(H(H(0\|\mathscr{B})\|\mathscr{L})\|\mathscr{O})\|\mathscr{A})$$

The application can generate secret data D_{secret} and seal it under the current value of PCR_5 by invoking:

$$\texttt{Seal}((5), D_{secret}) \rightarrow C = Enc_K((5, h)\|D_{secret})$$

where K is a storage key generated by the TPM. The resulting ciphertext C is returned to the software that invoked the seal operation. What benefit does this provide? If the same boot sequence is repeated (in other words, if the exact same BIOS, bootloader, OS and application are loaded in the same order) then clearly PCR_5 will take on the same value it had before. Thus a call to $\texttt{Unseal}$ will produce D_{secret}. However, if any of these pieces of software changes, then the $\texttt{Unseal}$ will fail. For example, suppose an attacker replaces the OS with a malicious OS ($\hat{\mathscr{O}}$). When the application is executed, the value of PCR_5 will be:

$$\hat{h} = H(H(H(H(0\|\mathscr{B})\|\mathscr{L})\|\hat{\mathscr{O}})\|\mathscr{A})$$

The properties of the hash function H guarantee that with extremely high probability $\hat{h} \neq h$, and thus if an attacker invokes $\texttt{Unseal}$, the TPM will refuse to decrypt C.

4 Can We Use Platform Information Remotely?

Section 2 described mechanisms for accumulating measurements of software state. In this section, we treat the issue of conveying these measurement chains to an external entity in an authentic manner. We refer to this process as *attestation*, though some works use the phrase *outbound authentication*. We also discuss privacy concerns and mitigation strategies that arise when sharing this information with third parties.

4.1 Prerequisites

The *secure boot* model (Section 3.1) does not capture enough information to securely inform a remote party about the current state of a computer, since it (at best), informs the remote party that the platform booted into some "authorized" state, but does not capture which state that happens to be, nor which values were considered during the authorization boot process.

Instead, a remote party would like to learn about the measurement of the currently executing code, as well as any code that could have affected the security of this code. Section 2 describes how a *trusted boot* process securely records this information in measurement chains (using either certificates or hashes).

4.2 Conveying Code Measurement Chains

The high-level goal is to convince a remote party (hereafter: verifier) that a particular measurement chain represents the software state of a remote device (hereafter: attestor). Only with an authentic measurement chain can the verifier make a trust decision regarding the attestor. A verifier's trust in an attestor's measurement chain builds from a hardware root of trust (Section 6). Thus, prerequisites for attestation are that the verifier (1) understands the attestor's hardware configuration and (2) is in possession of an authentic public key bound to the hardware root of trust.

The attestor's hardware configuration is likely represented by a certificate from its manufacturer, e.g., the IBM 4758's factory Layer 1 certificate [182], or the TPM's Endorsement, Platform, and Conformance Credentials [213]. Attestation-specific mechanisms for conveying public keys in an authentic way are treated with respect to privacy issues in Section 4.3. Otherwise, standard mechanisms (such as a Public Key Infrastructure) for distributing authentic public keys apply.

The process of actually conveying an authenticated measurement chain varies depending on the hardware root of trust. We first discuss a more general and more powerful approach to attestation used on general-purpose secure coprocessors such as the IBM 4758 family of devices. Then, given the prevalence of TPM-equipped platforms today, we discuss attestation as it applies to the TPM.

4.2.1 General Purpose Coprocessor-Based Attestation

Smith discusses the need for coprocessor applications to be able to authenticate themselves to remote parties [182]. This is to be distinguished from merely configuring the coprocessor as desired prior to deployment, or including a signed statement about the configuration. Rather, the code entity itself should be able to generate and maintain authenticated key pairs and communicate securely with any party on the Internet. Smith details the decision to keep a private key in tamper-protected memory and have some authority generate certificates about the corresponding public key. As these coprocessors are expensive devices intended for use in high assurance applications, considerably less attention has been given to the device identity's impact on privacy.

Naming code entities on a coprocessor is itself an interesting challenge. For example, an entity may go through one or more upgrades, and it may depend on lower layer software that may also be subject to upgrades. Thus, preserving desired security properties for code and data (e.g., integrity, authenticity, and secrecy) may depend not only on the versions of software currently running on the coprocessor, but also on past and even future versions. The IBM 4758 exposes these notions as *configurations* and *epochs*, where configuration changes are secret-preserving and epoch changes wipe all secrets from the device.

During a configuration change, certificate chains incorporating historical data are maintained. For example, the chain may contain a certificate stating the version of the lowest layer software that originally shipped on the device, along with a certificate for each incremental upgrade. Thus, when a remote party interacts with one of these devices, all information is available about the software and data contained within.

This model is a relative strength of general-purpose cryptographic coprocessors. TPM-based attestations (discussed in the next section) are based on hash chains accumulated for no longer than the most recent boot cycle. The history of software that has handled a given piece of sensitive data is not automatically maintained.

Smith examines in detail the design space for attestation, some of which is specific to the IBM 4758, but much of which is more generally applicable [182]. A noteworthy contribution not discussed here is a logic-based analysis of attestation. See Section 8 for additional work on validating the bootstrapping of trust.

4.2.2 TPM-Based Attestation

TPM-based attestation affords less flexibility than general coprocessor-based attestation, since the TPM is not capable of general-purpose computation. During the attestation protocol (shown in Figure 4), software on the attestor's computer is responsible for relaying information between the remote verifier and the TPM [213]. The protocol assumes that the attestor's TPM has generated an Attestation Identity Keypair (AIK), which is an asymmetric keypair whose public component must be known to the verifier in advance, and whose private component is only accessible to the TPM. We discuss privacy issues regarding AIKs in Section 4.3.1.

During the protocol, the verifier supplies the attestor with a nonce to ensure freshness (i.e., to prevent replay of old attestations). The attestor then asks the TPM to generate a *Quote*. The Quote is a digital signature covering the verifier's nonce and the current measurement aggregates stored in the TPM's Platform Configuration Registers (PCRs). The attestor then sends both the quote and an accumulated measurement list to the verifier. This measurement list serves to capture sufficiently detailed metadata about measured entities to enable the verifier to make sense of them. Exactly what this list contains is implementation-specific. Marchesini et al. focus on the measurement of a long-term core (e.g., kernel) [127], while IBM's Integrity Measurement Architecture contains the hash and full path to a loaded executable, and recursively measures all dynamic library dependencies [164]. To check the accuracy of the measurement list, the verifier computes the hash aggregate that would have been generated by the measurement list and compares it to the aggregate signed by the TPM Quote. This verification process involves efficient hash function computations, so it is more efficient than performing a public-key based certificate verification for every measurement.

Coker et al. [45] discuss five principles that should guide the development of attestation-based systems. In particular, they highlight the importance of freshness and the need for comprehensive information about the attestor. The latter creates tension with the attestor's need to limit the amount of information it discloses. They also argue that the semantics of an attestation should be made explicit, so that they can be subjected to formal logical analysis.

Preventing Reboot Attacks

A naive implementation of the above attestation protocol is susceptible to a *reboot* or *reset* attack. The basic weakness is a time-of-check to time-of-use (TOCTOU) vulnerability where the attesting platform is subject to remote physical tampering, such as power-cycling the platform. For example, the adversary may wait until the verifier has received an attestation, then reset the attestor and boot a malicious software image. Mitigating this attack requires a way to bind ephemeral session keys to the currently executing software [64, 75, 130]. These keys can then be used to establish a secure channel (see below). A reboot destroys the established tunnel, thereby breaking the connection and preventing the attack.

However, these defenses are insufficient to prevent slightly more sophisticated attacks that can be launched by an attacker in physical possession of the computer [102, 189]. By connecting the TPM's reset pin directly to ground, the attacker can reset the TPM independent of the rest of the platform. This causes the PCRs to reset and allows the attacker to extend arbitrary measurements into the PCRs and hence forge a set of measurements representing an arbitrary boot process. See Section 12.2 for discussion of other potential attacks.

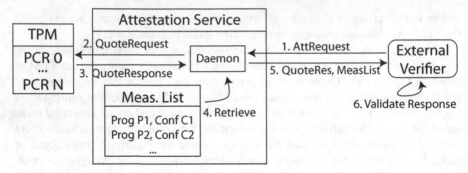

Fig. 4 Attestation. *High-level summary of a TPM-based attestation protocol using signed hash chain measurements [213], e.g., as in IBM's Integrity Measurement Architecture [164]. Some details are elided, e.g., the inclusion of an anti-replay nonce as part of the AttRequest message.*

Linking Code Identity to Secure Channels

Binding a secure channel (i.e., a channel that provides secrecy, integrity, and authenticity) to a specific code configuration on a remote host requires some care. Goldman et al. [75] consider an SSL client that connects to a server with attestation capabilities. Even if the client verifies the SSL certificate and the server's attestation, there is no linkage between the two. This enables an attack where a compromised SSL server forwards the client's attestation request to a different, trusted server. McCune et al. consider a similar challenge in establishing a secure channel between a client system and an isolated execution environment on a server [130, 131]. Both conclude that the solution is to include a measurement of the public key used to bootstrap the secure channel in the attestation, e.g., extend the public key into one of the TPM's PCRs. Goldman et al. also discuss other more efficient solutions in the context of a virtualized environment.

4.3 Privacy Concerns

Participating in an attestation protocol conveys to the verifier detailed information about the software loaded for execution on a particular platform. Furthermore, the attestation often depends on a cryptographic key embedded in the secure hardware, and using the same key in multiple attestations allows those attestations to be linked together.

In some cases, this may not be a concern. For example, in the military and in many enterprises, precise platform identification is desirable, and users do not have an expectation of privacy. As a result, some of the more expensive cryptographic co-processors that target these environments contain little provision for privacy.

However, in consumer-oriented applications, privacy is vital, and hence several techniques have been developed to maintain user privacy while still providing the ability to securely bootstrap trust.

4.3.1 Identity Certificate Authorities

One way to enhance user privacy is to employ a trusted third party to manage the relationship between a platform's true unique identity, and one or more pseudonyms that can be employed to generate attestations for different purposes. The Trusted Computing Group initially adopted this approach in the TPM [213], dubbing the trusted third party a *Privacy CA* and associating the pseudonyms with *Attestation Identity Keypairs* (AIKs). A TPM's true unique identity is represented by the *Endorsement Keypair* (EK) embedded in the TPM.[2]

At a high level, the trusted third party validates the correctness of the user's secure hardware, and then issues a certificate declaring the user's pseudonym corresponds to legitimate secure hardware. With the TPM, the user can ask the TPM to generate an arbitrary number of AIKs. Using the TPM's EK, the user can convince the Privacy CA to issue a certificate for the public portion of an AIK, certifying that the private portion of the AIK is known only to a real, standards-compliant TPM. Of course, for many applications, it will be necessary to use a consistent pseudonym for that particular application (e.g., online banking).

The Privacy CA architecture described above has encountered some real-world challenges. In reality, there is no one central authority trusted by all or even most users. Furthermore, a Privacy CA must be highly secure while also maintaining high availability, a nontrivial undertaking. To date, no commercial Privacy CAs are in operation, though a handful of experimental services have been created for research and development purposes [58, 157]. Pirker et al. implement their service in Java and make the code freely available [157].

4.3.2 Direct Anonymous Attestation

To address the limitations of Privacy CAs, a replacement protocol called Direct Anonymous Attestation (DAA) [23] was developed and incorporated into the latest TPM specification [213]. DAA is completely decentralized and achieves anonymity by combining research on group signatures and credential systems. Unlike many group signatures, it does not include a privileged group manager, so anonymity can never be revoked. However, it does allow membership to be revoked. In other words,

---

[2] It is possible to clear a TPM's EK and generate a new one. However, once an EK is cleared, it cannot be reinstated (the private key is lost). Further, high-quality TPMs ship from the manufacturer with a certified EK. Without a certified EK, it is difficult for a Privacy CA to make a trust decision about a particular TPM. Generating one's own EK is most appropriate for security-aware enterprises with procedures in place to generate new EKs in physically controlled environments, or for highly security-conscious individuals.

an adversary's credentials can be invalidated without the system ever actually learning the adversary's identity.

With DAA, a TPM equipped platform can convince an *Issuer* that it possesses a legitimate TPM and obtain a membership certificate certifying this fact. However, the interaction with the Issuer is performed via zero-knowledge proofs, so that even if the Issuer colludes with a verifier, the user's anonymity is protected.

DAA also allows a user to select any desired level of privacy by employing an arbitrarily large set of pseudonyms. Thus, the user can be anonymous (by using a new pseudonym for every attestation), fully traceable (by using a single fixed pseudonym), or any level of privacy in between. These pseudonyms can be used to authorize standard TPM AIKs, so existing techniques for attestation continue to function.

In practice, however, DAA has been slow to catch on. No currently available hardware TPMs offer DAA support, due in part to the cost of implementing expensive group signature operations on the limited TPM processor. The DAA algorithm is also quite complex, since it offloads as much computation as possible to the system's (relatively) untrusted primary CPU.

Rudolph noted some weaknesses in the original DAA design that could undermine its anonymity properties [160], primarily by having the Issuer employ different long-term keys for different users. Several fixes have been proposed [120], but these attacks highlight the ability of implementation "details" to undermine the security of formally proven systems.

More recently, researchers have pursued approaches to DAA that reduce the number of expensive computations that must be performed inside of the TPM [24, 37].

5 How Do We Make Sense of Platform State?

Knowing what code is executing on a platform does not necessarily translate into knowing whether that code can be trusted. In this section, we elaborate on this problem (5.1) and then review solutions that fall into two broad categories: solutions that provide only the identity of security-relevant code (5.2), and those that convey higher-level information (5.3).

5.1 Coping With Information Overload

At a high level, converting code identity into security properties is simply an exercise in software engineering. If we build perfectly secure software, then knowing this bulletproof code is running on a computer suffices to assure us that the computer can be trusted. Unfortunately, developing software with strong security properties, even minimal security kernels with limited functionality, has proven to be a daunting and labor-intensive task [5, 73, 101, 107].

As a result, most computers run a large collection of buggy, unverified code. Worse, both OS and application code changes rapidly over time, making it difficult to decide whether a particular version of software, combined with dozens of other applications, libraries, drivers, etc., really constitutes a secure system.

Below, we examine techniques developed to cope with this state-space explosion.

5.2 Focusing on Security-Relevant Code

One way to simplify the decision as to whether a computer is trustworthy is to only record the identity of code that will impact the computer's security. Reducing the amount of security-relevant code also simplifies the verifier's workload in interpreting an attestation. To achieve this reduction, the platform must support multiple privilege layers, and the more-privileged code must be able to enforce isolation between itself and less-privileged code modules. Without isolation, privilege-escalation attacks (recall Section 2.1) become possible, enabling malicious code to potentially erase its tracks.

While layering is a time-honored technique for improving security and managing complexity [73, 101], we focus on the use of layering to simplify or interpret information given to an external party about the state of the system.

Privilege Layering via the Operating System

Similar to the semantic attestation [85] technique discussed in Section 2.2, Marchesini et al. introduce a system [127] that uses privilege layering to simplify measurement information. Rather than target a language runtime (as in semantic attestation), they target a module in a trusted OS, and their approach mixes the trusted boot and secure boot processes described in Sections 2.1 and 3.1. The platform records the launch of a long-term core (an SELinux kernel in their implementation) which loads and verifies a policy file supplied by an administrator. The long-term core contains an *Enforcer* module that ensures that only applications matching the policy are allowed to execute. Thus, application execution follows the secure boot model. Secrets are bound to the long-term core, rather than specific applications, using trusted boot measurements as described in Section 3.2. If an external party can be convinced via remote attestation that the long-term core is trustworthy, then the only additional workload is to verify that the Enforcer is configured with an appropriate policy (i.e., one that satisfies the external party's requirements).

Jaeger et al. propose a similar system for enforcing a particular policy [97]. Their policy-reduced integrity measurement architecture (PRIMA) enforces an integrity policy called Clark Wilson-Lite (CW-Lite) [176]. CW-Lite relaxes the original Clark-Wilson [44] requirements that complete, formal assurance of programs is required, and that all interfaces must have filters. Instead, only interfaces accepting low-integrity inputs must have filters. PRIMA supports the notion of trusted and untrusted subjects, and extends IBM's IMA [164] to also measure the Mandatory Access Control (MAC) policy, the set of trusted subjects, and the code-subject mapping (e.g., the active user or role when a program is run). Verification of an attestation produced on a PRIMA-capable system involves additional checks. Verification fails if any of the following occur: (1) an untrusted program executes, or (2) a low integrity flow enters a trusted program without first being filtered. PRIMA is prototyped using SELinux.

Privilege Layering via Virtualization

The model of attesting first to a more-privileged and presumably trustworthy core, and then to only a portion of the environment running thereupon, has been explored in great detail in the context of virtualization.

One of the early designs in this space was Microsoft's Next-Generation Secure Computing Base (NGSCB) [42, 55]. With NGSCB, security-sensitive operations are confined to one virtual machine (VM), while another VM can be used for general-purpose computing. The VMM is trusted to provide strong isolation between virtual machines (VMs), and hence an external party need only learn about the identity of the VMM and a particular VM, rather than all of the code that has executed in the other VMs. Specifically, handoff attacks (Section 2.1) are significant only prior to the VMM itself launching, and within the VM where an application of interest resides. Handoff attacks in other VMs are irrelevant. The challenge remains to this day, however, to construct a VMM where privilege-escalation attacks are not a serious concern. The NGSCB architecture had a significant influence on the design of the TPM, DRTM (see Section 5.2), and early thinking on how to build secure applications on a bootstrapped foundation of trust [140].

Recording the initial VM image also provides a simple way of summarizing an entire software stack. With the advent of "virtual appliances," e.g., a dedicated banking VM provided by one's bank, this model can be quite promising. Terra generalized this approach to allow multiple "open", unrestricted VMs to run alongside "closed" or proprietary VMs [64]. sHype, from IBM, enforces mandatory access control (MAC) policies at the granularity of entire virtual machines [163]. Similar projects, including Nizza [179], Proxos [202], and Overshadow [41], have utilized virtualization to separate security-sensitive code from untrusted code. Unfortunately, the large Trusted Computing Base (TCB) of such solutions makes strong assurance difficult.

Schiffman et al. [169] describe a virtualization-based architecture for providing strong integrity assurances in a data center. A VM verifier checks the integrity of each application VM before executing it, and then an enforcer in each VMM imposes a variant of the Clark-Wilson integrity model [176] on the VMs as they execute. Traditional attestation mechanisms attest to the correct execution of the VMM, as well as the policies enforced. The system relies on a Root of Trust Installation (ROTI) mechanism [192] to bind the integrity of a privileged VM to the integrity of its installer. In other words, the integrity of a currently executing system can be tied back to the installer (e.g., a DVD ISO) that created the system, simplifying verification. One drawback of the ROTI approach is that it requires the system's persistent state to be largely static, as significant changes in the persistent state are difficult to map back to the original installation.

Hardware-Supported Isolation: System-Management Mode

Azab et al. [12] demonstrate how System-Management Mode (SMM) can be used to monitor and attest to the integrity of a hypervisor, without adding an additional layer of software "underneath" the hypervisor. SMM is a special x86 execution mode that is invoked via System-Management Interrupts (SMIs). SMM is often used to control fan speed or react to special keys on laptop keyboards (e.g., the volume control buttons). Code in an SMI handler operates independently of normal system code, such as the OS or hypervisor, and it can introspect on CPU state and the contents of memory. The HyperSentry system [12] uses a remote management interface to invoke an SMI and hence trigger their SMM-based checker. Examples of remote management interfaces include the Intelligent Platform Management Interface (IPMI) [91] and Intel's Active Management Technology (AMT), which is now a part of Intel's vPro Technology [94]. This ensures that any malware running in the OS or hypervisor will not know when the checker is triggered, and hence will not have the opportunity to hide itself.

In order to convey integrity information to a remote verifier, HyperSentry relies on a trusted boot process (see Section 2.1). The Core Root of Trust for Measurement (CRTM – a portion of the BIOS) measures the rest of the BIOS and extends the measurement into a PCR. The BIOS then measures HyperSentry's SMI handler, extends that measurement as well, and installs the handler. Finally, the handler generates a public-private keypair and extends the public portion into the TPM. As a result, a standard TPM-based attestation will convince a remote party that HyperSentry was installed correctly and will convey enough information to establish a secure channel to HyperSentry.

To perform an integrity measurement over the hypervisor, HyperSentry uses a number of clever tricks to run a measurement agent in the hypervisor's context in such a way that malware running with hypervisor privileges cannot evade, predict, or interfere with the measurement. HyperSentry can then use its private key to sign the resulting measurement and leave it to the untrusted code to convey the signed measurement and the TPM-based attestation to the remote verifier. Note that refusal to provide this information also serves as evidence that the hypervisor has been compromised.

The primary challenge to deploying an SMM-based system like HyperSentry is that commercial computers do not allow the installation of arbitrary SMI handlers. The HyperSentry team was able to work with a manufacturer to install a custom BIOS on their machine, but this option is not available on a typical computer.

Hardware-Supported Isolation: Dynamic Root of Trust for Measurement

A further challenge is that even VMM-based solutions include a considerable amount of non-security-relevant code, e.g., the BIOS, the boot loader, and various option ROMs. This code makes attestation challenging for several reasons. First, these code modules differ significantly across platforms or even across versions of the same platform, making it difficult for the recipient to assess the security of a particular software stack. Additionally, these entities are more privileged than the VMM (since they run before the VMM at the highest possible privilege level) and may be capable of undermining the VMM's ability to subsequently instantiate strong isolation between VMs. Finally, most of this legacy code was not designed to collect measurements, and hence must be updated to establish a proper static chain of trust. For example, most firmware for performing a PXE (network-based) boot does not include facilities for creating or storing measurements of the boot image obtained via the PXE protocol. Until this firmware is updated, the platform cannot perform a trusted boot or a secure boot via the PXE protocol.

To address these shortcomings, AMD and Intel extended the x86 instruction set to support a *dynamic root of trust for measurement* (DRTM – also known as *late launch*) operation with their respective Secure Virtual Machine (SVM) and Trusted eXecution Technology (TXT) (formerly codenamed LaGrande Technology) initiatives [3, 93]. Both AMD and Intel are shipping processors and chipsets with these capabilities; they can be purchased in commodity computers. At a high level, a DRTM operation essentially resets the CPU and memory controller to a known state, atomically measures a piece of code into the TPM, and begins executing the code in a hardware-protected environment.

In more detail, the key new feature offered by the *SKINIT* instruction on AMD (or *GETSEC[SENTER]* on Intel) is the ability to launch a Virtual Machine Monitor

(VMM) or Security Kernel at an arbitrary time (hence the colloquialism *late* launch) with built-in protection against software-based attacks. When a DRTM is invoked, the CPU's state is reset, and direct memory access (DMA) protections for a region of memory are enabled. The CPU measures the contents (e.g., executable code) in the memory region, extends the measurement into a PCR of the TPM, and begins executing the code. Essentially, DRTM provides many of the security benefits of rebooting the computer (e.g., starting from a clean-slate), while bypassing the overhead of a full reboot (i.e., devices remain enabled, the BIOS and bootloader are not invoked, memory contents remain intact, etc.).

We now describe AMD's implementation of DRTM, followed by Intel's differences in terminology and technique.

AMD SECURE VIRTUAL MACHINE (SVM).
To initiate a DRTM with AMD SVM, software in CPU protection ring 0 (e.g., kernel-level code) invokes the *SKINIT* instruction, which takes a physical memory address as its only argument. AMD refers to the memory at this address as the Secure Loader Block (SLB). The first two words (16-bit values) of the SLB are defined to be its length and entry point (both must be between 0 and 64 KB).

To protect the SLB launch against software attacks, the processor includes a number of hardware protections. When the processor executes an *SKINIT* instruction, it disables DMA to the physical memory pages comprising the SLB by setting the relevant bits in the system's Device Exclusion Vector (DEV). It also disables interrupts to prevent previously executing code from regaining control. Debugging access is also disabled, even for hardware debuggers. Finally, the processor enters flat 32-bit protected mode and jumps to the provided entry point.

AMD SVM also includes support for attesting to the proper invocation of the SLB. As part of the *SKINIT* instruction, the processor first causes the TPM to reset the values of the TPM's *dynamic* PCRs (i.e., PCRs 17–23) to zero,[3] and then transmits the (up to 64 KB) contents of the SLB to the TPM so that it can be measured (hashed) and extended into PCR 17. Note that software cannot invoke the command to reset PCR 17. The only way to reset PCR 17 is by executing another *SKINIT* instruction. Thus, future TPM attestations can include the value of PCR 17 to attest to the use of *SKINIT* and to the identity of the SLB loaded.

INTEL TRUSTED EXECUTION TECHNOLOGY (TXT – FORMERLY LT).
Intel's TXT is comprised of processor support for virtualization (VT-x) and Safer Mode Extensions (SMX) [93]. Newer systems also include Virtualization Technology for Directed I/O (VT-d). SMX provides support for dynamic root of trust in a manner similar to AMD's SVM, so we focus primarily on the differences between the two technologies. Instead of *SKINIT*, Intel introduced an instruction called *GETSEC*. *GETSEC* is a *leaf* instruction, and performs different operations depending on the value in general purpose register EAX. The leaf corresponding to AMD's *SKINIT* is *GETSEC[SENTER]*.

---

[3] A reboot of the platform sets the values of dynamic PCRs to −1, unlike with *static* PCRs, which are set to 0 during a reboot.

A DRTM invoked with *GETSEC[SENTER]* is comprised of two phases. First, an Intel-signed code module – called the Authenticated Code Module, or ACMod – must be loaded into memory. The platform's chipset verifies the signature on the ACMod using a built-in public key, extends a measurement of the ACMod into PCR 17, and finally executes the ACMod. The ACMod is then responsible for measuring the equivalent of AMD's SLB (which is called an MLE, i.e., a Measured, Launched Environment), extending the measurement into PCR 18, and then executing the code. In analogy to AMD's DEV protection, Intel protects the memory region containing the ACMod and the SLB from outside memory access using VT-d.[4] However, unlike the 64 KB protected by AMD's DEV, Intel's default DMA protections can be configured to include two arbitrary sized swathes of memory – one below 4 GB, and one above 4 GB.

As the OSLO bootloader project noted [102], DRTM allows the chain of trust described in Section 2.1 to be significantly shortened. One promising design is to launch a VMM, which prevents some kinds of malicious platform firmware from attacking the VMM.

BIND [177] combined DRTM with secure information about the launched code's inputs and outputs, hence providing a more dynamic picture to a remote party. Since it predated the arrival of actual hardware support, it lacked an implementation.

The Flicker project [130, 131] found that this approach could be extended even further to provide a secure execution environment *on demand*. It combined DRTM with sealed storage (see Section 3.2) and a carefully engineered kernel module to allow the currently executing environment to be temporarily paused while a measured and isolated piece of code ran. Once completed, the previous environment could be resumed and run with full access to the platform's hardware (and hence execute at native speed). This reduced the code identity conveyed to a third party to a tiny Flicker-supplied shim (potentially as little as 250 lines of code) and the security-relevant code executed with Flicker protections. However, the authors found that since the DRTM primitive had not been designed to support frequent or rapid invocation, it introduced context-switch overheads on the order of tens or hundreds of milliseconds for practical security-sensitive code. Nonetheless, relatively simple changes to the hardware could dramatically improve this performance [132].

Finally, the TrustVisor project [129] attempts to strike a middle ground by employing a minimalist hypervisor to provide DRTM-like functionality to applications, greatly minimizing context switch overhead as compared to Flicker. It also provides a higher-level, simplified interface to TPM-like functionality, such as sealing secrets to code identity.

TPM LOCALITY.
The dynamic root of trust mechanism described above depends in part on a TPM privilege facility called *locality*. Locality is primarily intended to support a hierarchy

---

[4] Early versions used a Memory Protection Table (MPT) that is now deprecated. Note that Intel has continued to evolve their platform's supported capabilities, and that things continue to change even at the time of this writing.

of system software operating at different privilege levels as well as different levels of trustworthiness (e.g., a hypervisor, an operating system, and various applications).

Certain TPM commands (most notably those that can reset the value of a Platform Configuration Register) are only permitted from a sufficiently privileged locality. The following table provides a brief overview of the PCRs that can be reset at each locality.

Locality	Resettable PCR(s)
None	N/A
0	N/A
1	PCR 20
2	PCRs 19–20
3	PCRs 18–20
4	PCRs 17–20

The implementation of locality is specific to the integration of the TPM with a host platform such as the PC Client platform [212]. On PCs, the locality of the current TPM command is determined by the memory-mapped address in the host system's physical memory space that is used to communicate the command to the TPM. For example, a TPM command sent using an address of the form $0xfed40xxx$ will be treated as a locality 0 command, while the same command sent using an address of the form $0xfed44xxx$ will be treated as a locality 4 command. The CPU and chipset prevent software from employing the $0xfed44xxx$ addresses. Only the CPU itself, while executing the *SKINIT* or *GETSEC[SENTER]* instruction, can generate commands with these addresses. The most privileged software on the PC (e.g., the hypervisor or OS) can access all localities less than 4,[5] and it may choose to restrict other software even further by using memory protections to restrict access to the relevant physical addresses.

Interested readers should refer to the appropriate platform-specific specification for full details on the locality mechanism (e.g., the PC Client Specific TPM Interface Specification [212]).

Slicing and Privilege Separation

A persistent challenge in trying to restrict one's focus to security-relevant code is that most software was written without meticulous attention to the principle of least privilege. As such, researchers have endeavored to automatically apply privilege separation to a legacy codebase, via tools such as PrivTrans [25]. PrivTrans leverages programmer annotations to automatically separate an existing program into privileged and unprivileged components. The authors compare their results against the manual privilege separation performed for the OpenSSH utility.

Program Slicing is useful in this context [204, 222], as it allows computation of the set of program statements that affect values at some point of interest. However,

---

[5] Intel TXT platforms reserve Locality 3 access exclusively for their Autheticated Code Modules (see Section 5.2).

existing slicing techniques do not necessarily provide guarantees about the confidentiality of sensitive data. Monate and Signoles introduce a source-to-source program slicing method that preserves the confidentiality of information [141].

5.3 Conveying Higher-Level Information

An orthogonal approach to interpreting code identity is to convert the information into a set of higher-level properties that facilitate trust judgements. This is typically accomplished either via code-level constraints or by outsourcing the problem to a third-party.

Code Constraints

As discussed in Section 2.2, multiple research efforts have studied mechanisms for applying static methods (e.g., via type checking [100] or inline reference monitors [56]) or dynamic methods (e.g., via hypervisors [172, 191], security kernels [105], or language runtimes [85]) for conveying information about software. Attesting to code identity allows an external party to verify that the running code has been appropriately transformed or that the dynamic checker was loaded correctly. This in turn assures the external party that the code has the property (or properties) provided by the transformation or checker.

Nauman et al. propose an attestation framework that enables an object owner to specify detailed usage control policies to be evaluated on a remote platform [144]. Attestation is leveraged to convey enforcement information between platforms, and allows a challenger to verify that object attribute update behavior and information flow behavior are in accordance with the appropriate policy.

Outsourcing

Another approach is to outsource the problem of interpreting code identity to a third party. Terra [64] took an initial step in this direction, as the authors suggest that clients obtain certificates from their software providers that map hash values to software names and/or versions. By including these certificates with their attestation, the client simplifies the verifier's interpretation task (i.e., the verifier no longer needs to have its own database for mapping hash values to software packages, assuming the verifier trusts the PKI used by the software vendors).

Subsequent work by Sadeghi and Stüble develops this idea much further [162]. They propose *property-based* attestation, with the goal of attesting whether a platform or an application fulfills the desired security requirements without revealing the specific software and hardware configuration. The client contacts a third-party who certifies that the client's software satisfies a much higher-level property, e.g., the client's software will never leak sensitive data. The client then presents this certificate to the verifier. Assuming the verifier trusts this third-party, it can easily conclude that the client possesses the certified property. In this way, verifiers are: unable to discriminate based on certain business considerations (e.g., OS or application software vendors), relieved of the burden of somehow ascertaining all known trusted configurations, and relieved of the burden of actually making a trust assessment of a given configuration. Unfortunately, most work in this area does not specify how the third party decides whether a particular piece of software provides a given property.

While similar in name, property-based attestation [162] and semantic attestation [85] are quite different. Property-based attestation [162] focuses on replacing the TPM's hash-based measurements with software properties certified by third parties. In particular, these software properties should be used, instead of a list of hashes, for conveying the state of the platform or the binding of secrets to a particular configuration. In contrast, semantic attestation [85] uses standard attestation techniques to report on the execution of a trusted language runtime (e.g., Java or .NET) and a (potentially dynamic) policy enforced by that runtime. Thus, semantic attestation is orthogonal to outsourcing and, in fact, has more in common with the privilege layering (via OS or VMM) techniques discussed above.

Chen et al. later proposed protocols [38] for combining property-based attestation with anonymity protocols similar to DAA (see Section 4.3.2). Kühn et al. extend the functionality of property-based attestation and construct a prototype on commodity systems [111]. Korthaus et al. describe an enhanced bootloader to support property-based attestation [109].

6 Roots of Trust

Trust in any system needs a foundation or a *root of trust*. Here, we discuss the roots of trust that have been proposed or deployed. Typically, the root of trust is based on the secrecy of a private key that is embedded in hardware; the corresponding public key is certified by the hardware's manufacturer. As we discuss, some systems further rely on a piece of code that must execute in the early boot process for their root of trust. We also discuss schemes where the root of trust is established by the properties of the physical hardware itself.

We defer to Sections 7 and 11 the discussion of how to create a *trusted path* between the human user and the root of trust. In brief, a trusted path is a mechanism for creating a secret and authenticated channel from the user to another entity, in this case the computer system's root of trust. It is intimately related to the user's mental model of the computer system. With a well-constructed trusted path, the user should know the identity of entity with which she communicates, that entity should "know" that the communications come from the user (and not from, e.g., other software), and the contents of the communication should remain secret and unmodified.

We divide this section as follows: 1) general-purpose devices with significant resistance to physical tampering, 2) general-purpose devices without significant physical defenses, 3) special-purpose minimal devices, and 4) research solutions that attempt to instantiate a root of trust without custom hardware support.

6.1 General-Purpose Tamper-Resistant and Tamper-Responding Devices

We first discuss commercial solutions available today. Relatively few products have achieved widespread commercial success, since tamper-resistant devices require costly manufacturing processes. We then discuss research projects that developed many of the design ideas manifested in today's commercial solutions. In all of these systems, the hardware stores a secret private key, and the manufacturer digitally signs a certificate of the corresponding public key. The certificate forms the root of trust that a verifier uses to establish trust in the platform.

6.1.1 Commercial Solutions

IBM offers a family of general-purpose cryptographic co-processors with tamper-resistant and tamper-responding properties, including the PCI-based 4758 [99, 184, 185] and the PCI-X-based 4764/PCIXCC [11, 89]. These devices include packaging for resisting and responding to physical penetration and fluctuations in power and temperature. Batteries provide power that enables an active response to detected tampering, in the form of immediate erasure of the area where internal secrets are stored and permanently disabling the device. Some of these devices include support for online battery replacement, so that the lifetime of these devices is not constrained by the lifetime of a battery.

Many higher-end smart cards and SIM cards include protections against physical attack. For example, the Infineon line of SLE88 chips includes sensors to detect voltage fluctuations, glitches, and light, as well as filters designed to smooth power usage (and hence frustrate power analysis) [90]. In these devices, a private key, typically used for authentication, resides solely in the microprocessor, and all private key operations take place within the microprocessor itself. Thus, the card can be used to interact with potentially untrusted terminals without risking key exposure. Gobioff et al. discuss the need for an on-card trusted path to the user, since an untrusted terminal can display some information to the user but perform a different transaction with the card itself (e.g., doubling the amount of a transaction) [71]. Smart cards are also discussed in Section 11.

6.1.2 Research Projects

μABYSS [221] and Citadel [223] are predecessors of the modern IBM designs, placing a CPU, DRAM, flash ROM, and battery-backed RAM (BBRAM) within a physically tamper-resistant package. Tampering causes erasure of the BBRAM, consequently destroying the keys required to decrypt the contents of DRAM. The Dyad secure co-processor [226] also presents some design elements visible today in IBM's devices. Only signed code from a trusted entity will be executed, and bootstrapping proceeds in stages. Each stage checks its integrity by comparing against a signature stored in the device's protected non-volatile memory.

The XOM [123] and AEGIS[6] [201] designs do not trust the operating system, and include native support for partitioning cache and memory between mutually distrusting programs. The AEGIS design [201] generates secrets (for use as encryption keys) based on the physical properties of the CPU itself (e.g., logic delays). Physical tampering will impact these properties, rendering the encryption keys inaccessible.

The Cerium processor design is an attempt at providing similar properties while remaining a largely open system [36]. Cerium relies on a physically tamper-resistant CPU with a built-in private key. This key is then used to encrypt sensitive data before it is sent to memory. Cerium depends on a trusted micro-kernel to manage address space separation between mutually distrusting processes, and to manage encryption of sensitive data while it resides in untrusted DRAM.

Lee et al. propose the Secret Protected (SP) architecture for virtual secure coprocessing [117]. SP proposes hardware additions to standard CPUs in the form of a small key store, encryption capabilities at the cache-memory interface, new instructions, and platform changes to support a minimalistic trusted path. These facilities

---

[6] Two relevant research efforts have used the name AEGIS. One is that of Arbaugh et al. [8] discussed in Section 2.1. The other is by Suh et al. [201] and is discussed in this section.

enable a Trusted Software Module to execute with direct hardware protection on the platform's primary CPU. This module can provide security-relevant services to the rest of the system (e.g., emulate a TPM's functionality), or it can implement application-specific functionality. Data is encrypted and integrity protected when it leaves the CPU for main memory, with the necessary keys residing solely within the CPU itself. SP pays considerable attention to the performance as well as security characteristics of the resulting design.

6.2 General-Purpose Devices Without Dedicated Physical Defenses

Here we discuss devices that are designed to help increase the security of software systems, but do not incorporate explicit physical defense measures. In practice, the degree of resilience to physical compromise varies widely. For example, consider the differences in physically attacking a device 1) on a daughter card that can be readily unplugged and interposed on, 2) soldered to the motherboard, 3) integrated with the "super-IO" chip, and 4) on the same silicon as the main CPU cores. The best examples for commodity platforms today are those equipped with a Trusted Platform Module (TPM), its mobile counterpart, the Mobile Trusted Module (MTM [53, 211]), or a smart card.

TPM-equipped Platforms

The TPM chip is a hardware device, but it does not employ any specific tamper resistance. Trust in the TPM stems from three roots of trust, specifically the roots of trust for Storage, Reporting, and Measurement. Trusted storage is provided by an encryption key that permanently resides within the TPM in nonvolatile RAM (see Section 3.2.2). The root for reporting (or communicating measurements to an external party) can be protected by the TPM's storage facilities. Finally, TPM measurement depends an immutable part of platform firmware called the Core Root of Trust for Measurement, which initializes the TPM when a platform first boots up.

MTM-equipped Platforms

The TCG Mobile Phone Working Group (MPWG) has specified a Mobile Trusted Module (MTM) [211]. The MTM specification interleaves two different profiles, depending on the device's owner: a Mobile *Local Owner* Trusted Module (MLTM) and a Mobile *Remote Owner* Trusted Module (MRTM). The local owner has physical control over the device, i.e., its user. The remote owner is a stakeholder without physical access to the deployed device, e.g., a device manufacturer or a network service provider.

In the MRTM (Remote Owner) profile, trust stems from four distinct roots of trust: Storage, Enforcement, Reporting, and Verification. These roots of trust represent security preconditions required for the MTM to initialize successfully [53]. Unlike the TPM, an MTM may be implemented entirely in software, although a device secret must be protected so that it can be used to provide a secure root of trust for storage facilities. Similar to the TPM, the other roots can use keys that are protected by secure storage. The root of trust for execution typically makes use of the isolated execution features of the platform's main CPU, e.g., ARM Trust-Zone [9] or TI M-Shield [13]. Boot integrity is provided using a *secure boot* model (Section 3.1).

Researchers are exploring this space. Winter details a design combining TCG and ARM TrustZone ideas for embedded Linux [224]. Ekberg and Bugiel present a software implementation of an MRTM, taking care to minimize its space constraints as far as possible [52]. This minimized MRTM is more easily realized on real-world secure execution environments with highly constrained memory resources, e.g., TI M-Shield as mentioned above. Dietrich et al. consider two approaches for providing modular, customizable MTM functionality which are based on currently available cell phones' security extensions – ARM TrustZone processor extensions and Secure Elements [47].

Bugiel and Ekberg extend the execution environment available to a protected software module (in the context of Flicker – Section 5.2) to include a full MTM [27]. They observe that modules that manage credentials will preserve the secrecy and integrity of the credentials, but that deployed credentials may still be misused (though not leaked) by other applications. Thus, an architecture is presented that is intended to provide the link between applications, their respective sealed credentials, and the secure execution environment.

Smart Cards

Unlike the high-end products discussed in Section 6.1.1, low-end smart cards and SIM cards may not have any active tamper response mechanisms; instead, they often attempt to protect a secret key through techniques such as hardware obfuscation [227].

6.3 Special-Purpose Minimal Devices

Several research projects have considered the utility of special-purpose security hardware. In general, this minimalistic approach works for some applications, but the limited functionality will exclude many applications that depend on reporting exactly what code is currently executing. Characterizing more precisely what functionality is needed in secure hardware for various classes of applications is still an open area of research.

Preventing Equivocation

Chun et al. observe that much of the complexity in Byzantine-Fault-Tolerant protocols arises from an adversary's ability to lie *differently* to each legitimate participant [43]. They show that the ability to attest to an append-only log can prevent such duplicity, and can hence greatly reduce the complexity and overhead of these protocols. Following up on this work, Levin et al. [121] show that the same property can be achieved with a much simpler primitive, namely the ability to attest to the value of a counter. They informally argue that this is the simplest primitive that can provide this property, and they show that an attested counter can be used in a range of applications, including PeerReview and BitTorrent.

Physical Unclonable Functions (PUFs)

Microscopic differences in manufacturing processes cause no two devices to be identical at the atomic level. Research in physical one-way functions [148], also known as physical unclonable functions, explores the applicability of such properties to security protocols. Circuits can be produced that are easy to evaluate but (it is hoped) practically impossible to predict or replicate. At the time of this writing PUFs remain a promising mechanism for providing strong device identity, which has applications in attestation protocols, e.g., [28, 118]. Schellekens et al. also typify this space by investigating trusted computing on low-cost reconfigurable hardware without non-volatile storage, such as low-end FPGAs, using a PUF to bootstrap key storage [168]. Recently, Armknecht et al. formalized a large collection of extant research on physical functions [10].

6.4 Research Solutions Without Hardware Support

The research community has proposed mechanisms to establish a software-based root of trust based solely on the properties of the physical hardware, i.e., without special hardware support. The key idea in *software-based attestation* is to have code compute a checksum over itself to verify its integrity [69, 104, 173, 174, 175, 190]. A verifier checks the result of the computed checksum and also measures the computation time. If an adversary interferes with the checksum computation, the interference will either slow the computation (and such timing deviation can be detected by the verifier) or will result in an incorrect checksum. Software-based attestation requires several strong assumptions, including the need for the verifier to have intimate knowledge of the hardware platform being verified, i.e., the verifier must know the platform's CPU make and model, clock speed, cache architecture, etc. In comparison with hardware-based techniques, the resulting security properties are similar to those of DRTM on a platform such as AMD SVM [3] or Intel TXT [93] (see Section 5.2). Secure storage remains a challenge as we discuss below.

The earliest proposal in this area is due to Spinellis [190], who proposes to use a timed self-checksumming code to establish a root of trust on a system. In the same vein, Kennel and Jamieson propose to use hardware side-effects to authenticate software [104]. Seshadri et al. implement a timed checksum function on embedded systems as well as on PCs [173, 174]. Shaneck et al. and Giffin et al. propose the use of self-modifying code to strengthen self-checksumming [69, 175].

Attacks have been proposed against weakened versions of software-based attestation mechanisms [32, 225]; however, these attacks are primarily based on implementation flaws, rather than fundamental limitations of the approach. Indeed, Perrig and van Doorn describe issues with some of the attacks [154]. Even so, additional formalism is needed to create true confidence in software-based attestation.

Long-term secure storage is also an open challenge for software-based attestation. This is because software-based attestation has no dedicated or hardware-protected storage for integrity measurements or secrets bound to integrity measurements. Thus, if such properties are desired, they must be engineered in software. However, there are fundamental limitations to the types of storage that can be protected long-term (e.g., across a power cycle) without a root of trust for storage (e.g., an encryption key available only to the trusted code that runs as part of the software-based attestation).

One line of research has avoided this dependence on hardware properties by focusing on auditing the results of specific function evaluations. Audit-based solutions [19, 142] typically require the client (or randomly selected workers) to recalculate some portion of the work done by untrusted workers. This may be infeasible for resource-constrained clients and often relies on some fraction of the workers to be honest, or at least non-colluding.

A variant on the logging approach depends on tamper-evident logs and deterministic replay [84]. Specifically, the authors propose a system to attest to the actions of a virtual machine (VM) without the need for hardware support. The VM runs atop an "Accountable VMM" that stores, in a tamper-evident log, all non-deterministic inputs to the VM, as well as all messages sent or received. When two parties interact, they exchange signed summaries of their logs, so that the each party can ensure the exchanged messages are properly logged. To verify Bob's VM, Alice requests a signed log of the VM's activity. Using her own reference implementation of the software allegedly running in the VM, Alice performs a deterministic replay of the inputs to the VM and verifies the output is consistent with the log.

Unlike typical bootstrapping approaches, the accountable replay approach does not report what software is actually running. As a result, it cannot prevent "enhancement" attacks. For example, one of the motivating examples the authors consider is gaming. An accountable VM would detect a user who installs software to give her infinite life, since this behavior is inconsistent with the behavior of the unmodified game. However, it would not detect cheating software that aims a gun for the player, or allows the player to see through walls. Cheats in this category produce VM output that is feasible within the unmodified game. In addition, efficiently performing deterministic replay is still quite challenging, particularly for multi-core systems [116].

7 Challenges in Bootstrapping Trust in Secure Hardware

Thus far, we have discussed how to use various secure hardware mechanisms to bootstrap trust in a platform, in particular by using the secure hardware to monitor and report on the software state of the platform. Given the software state, the user (or an agent acting on the user's behalf) can decide whether the platform should be trusted. Due to cost considerations, most commodity computers do not include a full-blown secure coprocessor such as the IBM 4758 [185]. Instead, the move has been towards cheaper devices such as the Trusted Platform Module (TPM) [213]. The cost reduction is due in part to the decision to make the TPM secure only against software attacks. As a consequence, a TPM in the physical possession of an adversary cannot be trusted.

With appropriate software support, the TPM can be used to measure and record each piece of software loaded for execution, and to securely convey this information (via an attestation) to a remote party [164, 213] (see Section 4). With hardware support for a *dynamic root of trust*, included in the most recent CPUs from AMD and Intel, the attestation from the TPM can be simplified to attest to the secure, isolated execution of a particular piece of software (see Section 5.1). With either approach, the resulting attestations can be verified by a user's trusted device, such as a cellphone or a special-purpose USB device [215]. Thus, the TPM can be used to establish trust in the software on a machine.

However, the question remains: How do we bootstrap trust in the TPM itself? Surprisingly, neither the TPM specifications nor the academic literature have considered this problem. Instead, it is assumed that the user magically possesses the TPM's public key. While this assumption dispenses with the problem, it does not truly solve it, since in real life the user does not typically receive authentic public keys out of the blue. Without the TPM's public key, the user cannot determine if she is interacting with the desired local TPM or with an adversarially-controlled TPM. For example, in a cuckoo attack, malware on the local machine may forward the user's messages to a remote TPM that the adversary physically controls. Thus, the user cannot safely trust the TPM's attestation, and hence cannot trust the computer in front of her.

As a result, as noted by Parno [149], we need a system to allow a conscientious user to bootstrap trust in the *local* TPM, so that she can leverage that trust to establish trust in the entire platform. [7]

In this section, we discuss the following topics: 1) we formally define (using predicate logic) the problem of bootstrapping trust in a platform, 2) we show how the model captures the cuckoo attack, as well as how it suggests potential solutions, 3) we give sample instantiations of each type of solution and discuss their advantages and disadvantages, and 4) we recommend improvements for future platforms that aspire to be trusted.

---

[7] The text in this section is adapted from Parno's work [149].

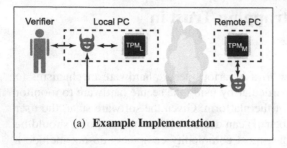
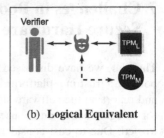

(a) **Example Implementation**   (b) **Logical Equivalent**

Fig. 5 The Cuckoo Attack. *In one implementation of the cuckoo attack (a), malware on the user's local machine sends messages intended for the local TPM (TPM_L) to a remote attacker who feeds the messages to a TPM (TPM_M) inside a machine the attacker physically controls. Given physical control of TPM_M, the attacker can violate its security guarantees via hardware attacks. Thus, at a logical level (b), the attacker controls all communication between the verifier and the local TPM, while having access to an oracle that provides all of the answers a normal TPM would, without providing the security properties expected of a TPM.*

7.1 Problem Definition

In this section, we present an informal description of the problem, followed by a more rigorous, formal definition.

We focus on a slightly abstracted model of the Trusted Platform Module (TPM). In particular, we model it as a security chip equipped with a public/private keypair $\{K_{TPM}, K_{TPM}^{-1}\}$ and a set of Platform Configuration Registers (PCRs). The TPM's manufacturer provides the TPM with an Endorsement Certificate, which certifies that the TPM is a genuine hardware TPM and serves to authenticate the TPM's public key K_{TPM}. Section 4.2.2 describes the lower-level details hidden by this abstraction.

7.1.1 Informal Problem Description

Our high-level goal is to establish trust in a potentially compromised computer, so that a user can perform security-sensitive tasks. To achieve this goal, we must assume the user already trusts someone or something, and then leverage that trust to establish trust in the computer.

Specifically, we make two initial trust assumptions. First, we assume the user has a mobile, trusted device, such as a cellphone, or a special-purpose USB device [215] that can compute and communicate with the computer. This device is assumed to be trusted in part due to its limited interface and functionality,[8] so it cannot be used for general security-sensitive tasks. We also assume the user trusts someone (potentially herself) to vouch for the physical integrity of the local machine. Without this assumption (which may not hold for kiosk computers), it is difficult to enable secure,

---

[8] Arguably, this assumption may not hold for current smartphones.

Predicates

Predicate	Meaning
TrustedPerson(p)	User trusts person p.
PhysSecure(c)	Computer c is physically secure.
SaysSecure(p, c)	Person p says computer c is physically secure.
Trusted$_C$(c)	Computer c is trusted.
Trusted$_T$(t)	TPM t is trusted.
On(t, c)	TPM t resides on computer c.
CompSaysOn(c, t)	Computer c says TPM t is installed on computer c.

Axioms

1. $\forall p,c$ TrustedPerson(p) $\land$ SaysSecure(p, c)
   $\rightarrow$ PhysSecure(c)
2. $\forall t,c$ On(t, c) $\land$ ¬ PhysSecure(c) $\rightarrow$ ¬ Trusted$_T$(t)
3. $\forall t,c$ On(t, c) $\land$ PhysSecure(c) $\rightarrow$ Trusted$_T$(t)

4. $\forall t,c$ On(t, c) $\land$ Trusted$_T$(t) $\rightarrow$ Trusted$_C$(c)
5. $\forall t,c$ On(t, c) $\land$ ¬ Trusted$_T$(t) $\rightarrow$ ¬ Trusted$_C$(c)

6. $\forall c,t$ CompSaysOn(c, t) $\rightarrow$ On(t, c)

Fig. 6 Trust Model. *The predicates describe relevant properties of the system, while the axioms encode facts about the domain.*

general-purpose computing. Fortunately, humans are relatively good at protecting their physical belongings (as opposed to virtual belongings, such as passwords). Furthermore, the assumption holds with respect to Internet-based attackers.

Ideally, from these two trust assumptions (a trustworthy verifier device and a physically secure local computer), we would establish trust in the secure hardware (TPM) in the local computer. Trust in the TPM could then be used to establish trust in the software on the computer. Unfortunately, there is currently no way to connect our trust assumptions to trust in the local TPM. When a user walks up to a computer, she has no reliable way of establishing the identity (public key) of the TPM inside the computer. As a result, she may fall victim to what we call a cuckoo attack.

In a *cuckoo attack*,[9] the adversary convinces the user that a TPM the adversary physically controls in fact resides in the user's own local computer. Figure 5(a) illustrates one possible implementation of the cuckoo attack. Malware on the user's local machine proxies the user's TPM-related messages to a remote, TPM-enabled machine controlled by the attacker. The attacker's TPM$_M$ can produce an Endorsement Certificate certifying that the TPM's public key K_{TPM_M} comes from an authentic TPM. The attacker's computer then faithfully participates in the TPM protocol, and it provides an attestation that trusted software has been loaded correctly.

---

[9] The cuckoo bird replaces other birds' eggs with its own. The victim birds are tricked into feeding the cuckoo chick as if it were their own. Similarly, the attacker "replaces" the user's trusted TPM with his own TPM, leading the user to treat the attacker's TPM as her own.

Assumption	Encoding
1. Alice trusts herself.	`TrustedPerson(Alice)`
2. Alice says her computer C is physically secure.	`SaysSecure(Alice, C)`
3. The adversary controls machine M containing TPM_M.	`On(TPM`$_M$`, M)`
4. M is not physically secure.	$\neg$ `PhysSecure(M)`
5. Malware on Alice's machine C causes it to say that TPM_M is installed on C.	`CompSaysOn(C, TPM`$_M$`)`

Fig. 7 Trust Model Assumptions. *We encode our assumptions about the situation in predicates.*

(1)	`TrustedPerson(Alice)`	Assumption 1
(2)	`SaysSecure(Alice, C)`	Assumption 2
(3)	`PhysSecure(C)`	Axiom 1: (1), (2)
(4)	`CompSaysOn(C, TPM`$_M$`)`	Assumption 5
(5)	`On(TPM`$_M$`, C)`	Axiom 6: (4)
(6)	`Trusted`$_T$`(TPM`$_M$`)`	Axiom 3: (5), (3)
(7)	`Trusted`$_C$`(C)`	Axiom 4: (5), (6)
(8)	`On(TPM`$_M$`, M)`	Assumption 3
(9)	$\neg$ `PhysSecure(M)`	Assumption 4
(10)	$\neg$ `Trusted`$_T$`(TPM`$_M$`)`	Axiom 2: (8), (9)
(11)	$\neg$ `Trusted`$_C$`(C)`	Axiom 5: (5), (10)
(12)	$\bot$	7, 11

Fig. 8 Proof Failure Reveals Cuckoo Attack. *Applying our axioms to our assumptions leads to a logical contradiction.*

As a result, the user will decide to trust the local PC. Any secrets she enters can be captured by malware and forwarded to the attacker. Even secrets protected by TPM-based guarantees (e.g., encrypted using K_{TPM_M}) will be compromised, since the TPM's specifications offer no guarantees for a TPM in the physical possession of the adversary.

Thus, it is crucial that the user be able to securely communicate with the TPM in the *local* machine before revealing any sensitive information. Note that while this attack resembles a classic Attacker-in-the-Middle attack, it differs in that the attacker controls the software of the local machine and the hardware and software on the remote machine.

7.1.2 Formal Model

To analyze the cuckoo attack more formally, we can model the situation using predicate logic. Figure 6 summarizes our proposed model for establishing trust in a computer equipped with secure hardware. The first axiom encodes our assumption that trusted humans can vouch for the physical integrity of a computer. The next two axioms codify the TPM's vulnerability to hardware attacks. The second set of axioms encodes our assumption that trust in the TPM inside a computer suffices (via software attestations) to establish trust in the computer. The final axiom represents the fact that today, without the local TPM's public key, the user must accept the computer's assertion that a particular TPM resides on the computer.

To "initialize" the system, we also encode our assumptions about the concrete setting in a set of predicates (shown in Figure 7). By applying our set of axioms to the initial assumptions, we can reason about the trustworthiness of the local machine. Unfortunately, as shown in Figure 8, such reasoning leads to a logical contradiction, namely that the local machine C is both trusted and untrusted. This contradiction captures the essence of the cuckoo attack, since it shows that the user cannot decide whether to trust the local machine.

Removing the contradiction requires revisiting our axioms or our assumptions. We explore these options below.

7.2 Potential Solutions

The cuckoo attack is possible because the attacker can convince the user to accept assurances from an untrustworthy TPM. In this section, we first show that an obvious solution, cutting off network access, addresses one instantiation of the cuckoo attack but does not solve the problem, since malware on the local machine may have enough information to perfectly emulate a TPM in software. To avoid similar missteps, we return to our formal model and consider solutions that remove an assumption, as well as solutions that fix an axiom. For each approach, we provide several concrete instantiations and an analysis of their advantages and disadvantages.

7.2.1 Removing Network Access

From Figure 5(a), it may seem that the cuckoo attack can be prevented by severing the connection between the local malware the adversary's remote PC. The assumption is that without a remote TPM to provide the correct responses, the infected machine must either refuse to respond or allow the true TPM to communicate with the user's device (thus, revealing the presence of the malware).

Below, we suggest how this could be implemented, and show that regardless of the implementation, this solution fundamentally does not work. We demonstrate this both with the formal model from Section 7.1.2, and with an attack.

There are several ways to remove the local malware's access to the remote TPM. We could instruct the user to sever all network connections. If the user cannot be trusted to reliably accomplish this task,[10] the verifier could jam the network connections. For example, the user's trusted device might include an RJ-45 connector to plug the Ethernet jack and jam the wireless network at the logical level (by continuously sending Request-to-Send frames) or at the physical level. Finally, we could use a distance-bounding protocol [22] to prevent the adversary from making use of a remote TPM. Since the speed of light is constant [51], the verifier can require fast responses from the local platform and be assured that malware on the computer does not have time to receive an answer from a remote party. However, with current TPMs, identification operations take half a second or more, with considerable variance both on a single TPM and across the various TPM brands [132]. A signal traveling at the speed of light can circle the earth about four times in the time required for an average TPM to compute a signature, making distance-bounding infeasible.

Unfortunately, removing network access is fundamentally insufficient to prevent the replay attack. One way to see this is via the formal model from Figure 6. Neither the predicates nor the axioms assume the local adversary has access to the remote PC. The logical flaw that allows the cuckoo attack to happen arises from Axiom 6, i.e., the local computer's ability to convince the user that a particular TPM resides on the local computer. In other words, as shown in Figure 5(b), the cuckoo attack is possible because the malware on the local machine has access to a "TPM oracle" that provides TPM-like answers without providing TPM security guarantees. If the local malware can access this oracle without network access, then cutting off network access is insufficient to prevent the cuckoo attack.

In particular, since the adversary has physical possession of TPM_M, he can extract its private key. He can then provide the malware on the local computer with the private key, TPM_M's Endorsement Certificate, and a list of trusted PCR values. Thus provisioned, the malware on the local machine can perfectly emulate TPM_M, even without network access.

7.2.2 Eliminating Malware

An alternate approach is to try to remove the malware on Alice's local computer. In our formal model, this equates to removing Assumption 5, which would remove the contradiction that results in the cuckoo attack. Unfortunately, this approach is both circular and hard to achieve.

First, we arrived at the cuckoo attack based on the goal of ensuring that the local machine could be trusted. In other words, the goal is to detect (and eventually remove), any malware on the machine using the TPM. Removing malware in order to communicate securely with the TPM, in order to detect and remove malware, potentially leaves us stuck in an endless loop.

---

[10] For example, it may be difficult to tell if an infected laptop has its wireless interface enabled.

In practice, there are two approaches to cutting through this circularity, but neither is entirely satisfactory.

§1 **Trust.** The "null" solution is to simply ask the local machine for its key and trust that no malware is present.
Pros: This is clearly the simplest possible solution. Sadly, it seems to be the only viable solution available today, at least without special devices or additional hardware changes.
Cons: The assumption that the machine is not compromised will not hold for many computers. Unprotected Windows PCs are infected in minutes [2]. Even newly purchased devices may not meet this criteria [115, 186].

§2 **Timing Deviations.** Researchers have observed that certain computations can be done faster locally than malware can emulate the same computations while hiding its own presence (see Section 6.4). By repeating these computations, a timing gap appears between a legitimate execution of the protocol, and a malware-simulated execution. Using such a system, we could run a code module on the local computer to check for malware.
Pros: Since these approaches do not rely on special hardware, they can be employed immediately on current platforms.
Cons: Using timing deviations requires severing the PC's network access; Section 7.2.1 shows that this is non-trivial. Also, such techniques require specific hardware knowledge (e.g., about the exact CPU architecture/model, memory size, cache size, etc.) that the user is unlikely to possess.

7.2.3 Establishing a Secure Channel

Given the conclusions above, we must keep the assumptions in Figure 7. Thus, to find a solution, we must fix one or more of our axioms. We argue that the correct target is Axiom 6, as the others are fundamental to our problem definition.

We cannot simply remove Axiom 6, since without it, we cannot introduce the notion of a TPM being installed on a computer. Instead, establishing a secure (authentic and integrity-preserving) channel to the TPM on the local machine suffices to fix Axiom 6. Such a secure channel may be established using hardware or cryptographic techniques.

For a hardware-based approach, we would introduce predicate $HwSaysOn(t, c)$ to indicate that a secure hardwired channel allowed the user to connect to the TPM on the local machine. Axiom 6 would then be written as:

$$\forall t, c \quad HwSaysOn(t, c) \rightarrow On(t, c)$$

A cryptographic approach requires the user to obtain some authentic cryptographic information about the TPM she wishes to communicate with. Based on the user's trust in the source of the information, she could then decide that the TPM was in fact inside the machine. We could encode this using the predicate $PersonSaysOn(p, t, c)$ indicating that a person p has claimed that TPM t

is inside computer c. Axiom 6 would then be written as:

$$\forall p,t,c \quad \texttt{TrustedPerson}(p) \wedge \texttt{PersonSaysOn}(p,t,c) \rightarrow \texttt{On}(t,c)$$

Hardware-Based Secure Channels

Below, we analyze ways to implement a hardware-based modification to Axiom 6 to allow the user to establish a secure channel with the TPM on the local computer.

§3 **Special-Purpose Interface.** Add a new hardware interface to the computer that allows an external device to talk directly to the TPM. The TPM already supports differential access rights, so the external interface could be designed to allow the external verifier to guarantee that software on the machine does not interfere with the contents of the TPM while the verifier is attached.

Pros: The use of a special-purpose port reduces the chances for user error (since they cannot plug the external verifier into an incorrect port).

Cons: Introducing an entirely new interface and connector specification would require significant industry collaboration and changes from hardware manufacturers, making it an unlikely solution in the near term.

§4 **Existing Interface.** Use an existing external interface (such as Firewire or USB) to talk directly to the TPM.

Pros: This solution is much simpler to deploy, since it does not require any manufacturer changes.

Cons: Existing interfaces are not designed to support this type of communication. For example, USB devices cannot communicate with the host platform until addressed by the host. Even devices with more freedom, such as Firewire devices, can only read and write to memory addresses. While the TPM is made available via memory-mapped I/O ports, these mappings are established by the software on the machine, and hence can be changed by malware. Thus, there does not appear to be a way to reuse existing interfaces to communicate reliably with the local TPM.

§5 **External Late Launch Data.** Recent CPUs from AMD and Intel can perform a *late launch* of an arbitrary piece of code (see Section 5.1). During the late launch, the code to be executed is measured and the measurement is sent to the TPM. The code is then executed in a protected environment that prevents interference from any other hardware or software on the platform. If the late launch operation also made the code's measurement code available externally, then the user's verifier could check that the invoked code was trustworthy. The code could then check the integrity of the platform or establish a secure channel from the verifier to the TPM.

Pros: Recent CPUs contain the late launch functionality needed to measure and securely execute code.

Cons: Existing interfaces (such as USB) do not allow the CPU to convey the fact that a late launch occurred nor the measurement of the executed code in an authentic fashion. Malware on the computer could claim to perform a late launch and then send a measurement of a legitimate piece of code. This attack could be prevented by creating a special-purpose interface that talks directly to the CPU, but this brings us back to §3, which is a simpler solution.

§6 **Special-Purpose Button.** Add a new button on the computer for bootstrapping trust. For example, the button can execute an authenticated code module that establishes a secure channel between the verifier (connected via USB, for example) and the TPM. Alternatively, the button could disable all network interfaces to prevent the cuckoo attack from occurring. Such a button could also be useful for taking a laptop on an airplane.

Pros: A hardware button press cannot be overridden by malware. It also provides the user with a tangible guarantee that secure bootstrapping has been initiated.

Cons: Executing an authenticated code module requires hardware not only for invoking the necessary code, but also for verifying digital signatures (similar to §9), since the code will inevitably need updates. This approach also relies on the user to push the button before connecting the verifier device, since the device cannot detect the button push. If the user plugs in the verifier before pushing the button, on the computer could fool the device with a cuckoo attack. Both versions of this solution require hardware changes.

Cryptographic Secure Channels

Establishing a cryptographically-secure channel requires the user to share a secret with the TPM or to obtain the TPM's public key. Without a prior relationship with the TPM, the user cannot establish a shared secret, so in this section we focus on public-key methods.

§7 **Camera-based Channel.** Seeing-is-Believing (SiB), an approach suggested by McCune et al. [133] (and later used for kiosk computing [66]), requires the computer's manufacturer to encode a hash of the platform's identity in a 2-D barcode and attach the barcode to the platform's case. Note that this step should be performed by the manufacturer and not, say, the current owner, since the current owner would have to establish the TPM's identity, in which case the problem would simply recurse to them. Using a camera-equipped smartphone, the user can take a picture of the 2-D barcode and use the smartphone to process the computer's attestation.

Pros: This solution is attractive, since it requires relatively little effort from the manufacturer, and most people find picture-taking simple and intuitive.

Cons: Because it requires a vendor change, this solution will not help current platforms. It also requires the user to own a smartphone and install the relevant software. The user must also trust that the smartphone has not been compromised. As these phones grow increasingly complex, this assumption is likely to be violated. In a kiosk setting, the 2-D barcode may be replaced or covered up by an attacker.

§8 **Human-based Channel.** Instead of using a 2-D barcode, the manufacturer could encode the hash as an alpha-numeric string. The user could then enter this string into a smartphone, or into a dedicated trusted device.

Pros: Similar to §7, except the user no longer needs a camera-equipped device.

Cons: Similar to those of §7, but it still requires non-trivial input capability on the user's device. It also relies on the user to correctly enter a string of digits meaningless to the user.

§9 **Trusted BIOS.** If the user trusts the machine's BIOS, she can reboot the machine and have the trusted BIOS output the platform's identity (either visually or via an external interface, such as USB). The trusted BIOS must be protected from malicious updates. For example, some Intel motherboards will only install BIOS updates signed by Intel [113].

Pros: This approach does not require the user to use any custom hardware.

Cons: The user must reboot the machine, which may be disruptive. It relies on the user to only insert the verifier after rebooting, since otherwise the verifier may be deceived by local malware. The larger problem is that many mother-boards do not include the protections necessary to guarantee the trustworthiness of the BIOS, and there is no indicator to signal to the user that the BIOS in the local computer is trustworthy.

§10 **Trusted Third Party.** The TPM could be equipped with a certificate provided by a trusted third party associating the TPM with a particular machine. The verifier can use the trusted third party's public key to verify the certificate and establish trust in the TPM's public key.

Pros: The verifier only needs to hold the public key for the trusted third party and perform basic certificate checks. No hardware changes are needed.

Cons: It is unclear how the verifier could communicate the TPM's location as specified in the certificate to the user in a clear and unambiguous fashion. Bind-ing the certificate to the computer's serial number (or other information printed on a label attached the computer) has the same advantages and disadvantages as §8. This solution also moves the problem of establishing a TPM's identity to the third party, who must then employ one of the other solutions suggested here.

7.3 Preferred Solutions

Of all the solutions presented in Section 7.2, we argue that §3 (a special-purpose hardware interface) provides the strongest security. It removes almost every oppor-tunity for user error, does not require the preservation of secrets, and does not re-quire software updates. Unfortunately, the cost and industry collaboration required to introduce a new interface make it unlikely to be deployed in the near future.

Of the plausibly deployable solutions, we argue in favor of §8 (an alphanumeric hash of the TPM's public key), since it allows for a simpler verification device. Nonetheless, we recognize that these selections are open to debate, and believe that considerable room remains for additional solutions.

8 Validating the Process

Bootstrapping trust can only be effective if we can validate the hardware, software, and protocols involved. Below we summarize the (relatively few) efforts in this direction.

From a hardware perspective, Smith and Austel discuss efforts to apply formal methods to the design of secure coprocessors [180, 184]. They also state formal security goals for such processors. Bruschi et al. use a model checker to find a replay attack in the TPM's Object Independent Authorization Protocol (OIAP) [26]. They also propose a countermeasure to address their attack, though it requires a TPM design change.

Taking a more empirical approach, Chen and Ryan identify an opportunity to perform an offline dictionary attack on weak TPM authorization data, and propose fixes [39]. Sadeghi et al. performed extensive testing on TPMs from multiple vendors to evaluate their compliance with the specification [161]. They find a variety of violations and bugs, including some that impact security. Starting from the TPM specification, Gürgens et al. developed a formal automata-based model of the TPM [83]. Using an automated verification tool, they identify several inconsistencies and potential security problems. Shubina et al. study the development challenges created by TPM diversity, using as a case study their efforts to integrate the TPM into OpenSolaris [178].

Dwoskin et al. describe an informal framework, based on virtualization, for testing security architectures [49]. One VM hosts the test system, while another VM hosts the test framework and utilizes hooks in the VMM and in the test system to launch various simulated attacks. The VMM can also emulate new security hardware. For example, the authors emulate the SP architecture [117] (see Section 6.1.2). This allows them to discover, for example, that the secure load/store instructions significantly complicate the architecture. They replace the instructions with "secure areas", but the framework finds several issues with the implementation, including leakage of data on the stack and issues with pushing exception frames onto the stack.

At the software level, Kauer notes several implementation flaws in trusted computing applications [102]. These include bootloaders that fail to appropriately measure software before loading it, and BIOS software that allows flash updates without validation.

At the protocol layer, Smith defines a logic for reasoning about the information that must be included in platform measurements to allow a verifier to draw meaningful conclusions [182]. Millen et al. [139] use a symbolic model checker to verify the properties of a TPM-based measured boot, as well as those of a dynamic root of trust (see Section 5.2). They conclude that on Intel systems, finding the expected measurements of a hypervisor (or kernel) in PCRs 17 and 18 is sufficient to guarantee said hypervisor has been loaded, as long as the hypervisor is self-protecting. They also confirm that this guarantee is not impacted by the security (or insecurity) of software that runs earlier in the boot cycle, e.g., the BIOS or boot loader.

Datta et al. later used the Logic of Secure Systems (LS^2) [46] to formally define and prove the code integrity and execution integrity properties of the static and dynamic TPM-based attestation protocols. The logic also helps make explicit the invariants and assumptions required for the security of the protocols. For example, it is possible to lose information about the static root of trust when invoking dynamic root of trust multiple times. Systems must be explicitly engineered to maintain measurement chains across dynamic roots of trust.

9 Applications

Clearly, many applications benefit from the ability to bootstrap trust in a computer. Rather than give an exhaustive list, we focus on applications deployed in the real world, and a handful of particularly innovative projects in academia.

9.1 Real World

Code Access Security in Microsoft .NET

Microsoft's Code Access Security is intended to prevent unauthorized *code* from performing privileged actions [137]. The Microsoft .NET Common Language Runtime (CLR) maintains *evidence* for *assemblies* of code and uses these to determine compliance with a security policy. One form of evidence is the cryptographic hash of the code in question. This represents one of the more widely deployed systems that supports making security-relevant decisions based purely on the identity of code as represented by a cryptographic hash of that code.

BitLocker

One of the most widely-used applications of trust bootstrapping is BitLocker [138], Microsoft's drive encryption feature, which first appeared in the Windows Vista OS. Indeed, BitLocker's dependence on the presence of a v1.2 TPM likely helped encourage the adoption of TPMs into the commodity PC market. The keys used to encrypt and authenticate the harddrive's contents are sealed (see Section 3.2) to measurements taken during the computer's initial boot sequence. This ensures that malware such as boot-sector viruses and rootkits cannot hijack the launch of the OS nor access the user's files. These protections can be supplemented with a user-supplied PIN and/or a secret key stored on a USB drive.

The high profile of BitLocker has attracted the attention of multiple researchers. Türpe et al. show that (without compromising the cryptography or sealed storage primitives employed in BitLocker) the real-world attack surface includes such things as spoofing the unlock prompt or simply compromising some of BitLocker's executable files and hoping that the user will employ one of the non-TPM recovery mechanisms when the attack is detected, instead of taking the system in for servicing [214]. In one sense, this is a success on the part of BitLocker, since attackers' best options have been pushed towards tricking the human user. However, it remains an open question if a system can be constructed with similar technical security properties that has fewer opportunities to fool the user.

Trusted Network Connect (TNC)

TNC is a working group with goals including strengthening network endpoints. TNC supports the use of attestation to perform Network Access Control. Thus, before a computer can connect to the network, it must pass integrity checks on its software stack, as well as perform standard user authentication checks. An explicit goal is to give non-compliant computer systems an avenue for remediation. Existing open source solutions have already been tested for interoperability with promising results [87].

Secure Boot on Mobile Phones

Mobile phones (and other embedded devices) have long benefitted from a secure boot architecture. Until recently, these devices served very specific purposes, and the degree of control afforded to mobile network operators by a secure boot architecture helped to ensure dependable service and minimize fraud. Even many modern smartphones with support for general-purpose applications employ rich capability-based secure architectures whose properties stem from secure boot. For example, Symbian Signed [53] is the interface to getting applications signed such that they can be installed and access certain capabilities on smartphones running the Symbian OS. Apple's iPhone OS employs a similar design.

Voting Machines

With the recent move towards digital voting machines, techniques for bootstrapping trust in both the hardware and software employed become even more important. Gallo et al. [63] detail the software and hardware mechanisms employed in the design of over 165,000 direct-recording voting machines in Brazil's 2010 elections. While inspired in part by TPM-based designs, they design their system to employ active security measures to ensure that only signed code runs. A three-pronged certificate hierarchy separates the privileges needed for servicing and programming the machines from the privileges needed to record votes. The machine displays its current trust state via a set of LEDs, and poll workers can verify hardware integrity via a set of challenge-response values provided by the electoral commission. The voting machine responds to the challenges based on an internal, cryptographic identity key that should be destroyed if the processor is tampered with. The processor is a standard microcontroller enhanced with a variety of hardware defenses against physical tampering.

9.2 Research Proposals

Multiple projects have considered using secure hardware to bootstrap trust in a traditional "Trusted Third Party". Examples include certifying the behavior of the auctioneer in an online auction [155], protecting the private key of a Certificate Authority [130], protecting the various private keys for a Kerberos Distribution Center [95].

Given the ever increasing importance of web-based services, multiple research efforts have studied how to bootstrap greater assurance in public web servers. In the WebALPS project, building on the IBM 4758, Jiang et al. enhanced an SSL server to provide greater security assurance to a web client [98, 181]. A "guardian" program running on the secure coprocessor provides data authenticity and secrecy, as well as safeguarding the server's private SSL keys. This approach helps protect both the web client and the web server's operator from insider attacks. In the Spork project, Moyer et al. consider the techniques needed to scale TPM-based attestation to support a high-performance web server [143]. They also implement their design by modifying the Apache web server to provide attested content and developing a Firefox extension for validating the attestations.

Of course, other network protocols can benefit from bootstrapped trust as well. For example, the Flicker project (see Section 5.2) enhanced the security of SSH passwords while they are handled by the server. With a Flicker-enhanced SSH server, the client verifies an attestation that allows it to establish a secure channel to an isolated code module on the server. By submitting its password over this channel, the client can ensure that only a tiny piece of code on the server will ever see the password, even if other malware has infected the server. On a related note, the BIND project [177] observed that by binding bootstrapped code to its inputs, they could achieve a transitive trust property. For example, in the context of BGP, each router can verify that the previous router in the BGP path executed the correct code, made the correct decisions given its input, and *verified the same information about the router before it*. The last property ensures that by verifying only the previous router in the chain, the current router gains assurance about the entire BGP path. Keller, Lee, and Rexford explore this idea further in the context of hosted virtual networks [103]. In particular, they examine the tradeoffs involved in equipping routers with a TPM or an SP processor (see Section 6). Their primary goal is to enable a service provider to lease virtual routers from an infrastructure provider who installs and multiplexes physical routers. The service provider requires proof that her software is running correctly in the hosted environment.

Researchers have also investigated the use of bootstrapped trust in the network itself. Ramachandran et al. propose imbuing packets with the provenance of the hosts and applications that generated them [159]. Unfortunately, these packet markings are not secured, so the system must assume that the entire network is trusted and that all hosts have deployed the system in a tamper-proof fashion. Garfinkel et al. noted that secure hardware might help defend against network-based attacks [65].

However, the first design and implementation of this idea came from Baek and Smith, who describe an architecture for prioritizing traffic from privileged applications [14]. Using a TPM, clients attest to the use of an SELinux kernel equipped with a module that attaches Diffserv labels to outbound packets based on an administrator's network policy. This system requires a large TCB (i.e., an entire Linux kernel) and universal deployment. Gummadi et al. propose the Not-A-Bot system [82], which tries to distinguish human-generated traffic from bot-driven traffic. They attest to a small client module that tags outgoing packets generated within one second of a keystroke or mouse click. Through trace-driven experiments, the authors show that the system can significantly reduce malicious traffic. However, the system only considers application-level attacks, i.e., the network is assumed to be uncongested. Thus, the server is responsible for verifying client attestations, which is less practical for applications such as combating network-level DDoS attacks or super-spreader worms. The system works well for human-driven application-specific scenarios, but it is difficult to adapt it to services that are not primarily human-driven, such as NTP, transaction processing, network backup, or software update servers.

Rather than use a TPM, Feng and Schluessler propose, at a high level, using Intel's Active Management Technology to provide information on the machine's state to network elements by introspecting on the main CPU's activities [57]. They do not focus on conveying this information efficiently, nor do they provide a full system design and implementation. In a more orthogonal direction, Dixon et al. propose pushing middle-box functionality, such as NAT and QoS to endhosts, using trusted computing as a foundation [48].

Parno et al. [150, 153] propose a generic framework for efficiently conveying trustworthy host-based information to network elements. They explore how bootstrapping trust in endhosts (via techniques like those described in this work) can simplify network protocols or improve their efficiency. In their architecture, senders employ secure hardware to convince an off-path *verifier* that they have installed a small code module that maintains network-relevant information. A small protection layer enforces mutual isolation between the code module and the rest of the sender's software, ensuring both security and privacy. Once authorized by a verifier, the code module can insert cryptographically-secured information into outbound traffic. This information is checked and acted on by in-path *prioritizers*. The authors evaluate the effectiveness of this architecture for combatting spam, mitigating network-level distributed denial-of-service attacks, and detecting super-spreader worms.

Sarmenta et al. observe that a trusted monotonic counter can be used in a wide variety of applications, including count-limited objects (e.g., keys that can only be used a fixed number of times), digital cash, and replay prevention [165]. While the TPM includes monotonic counter functionality, the specification only requires it to support a maximum of four counters, and only one such counter need be usable during a particular boot cycle. Thus, they show how to use a log-based scheme to support an arbitrary number of simultaneous counters. They also design a more efficient scheme based on Merkle trees [136], but this scheme would require modifications to the TPM, so that it could securely store the tree's root and validate updates to it.

Schwartz et al. show how to provide a *contractual* anonymity system called RECAP by leveraging a trusted execution environment and a group signature scheme [171]. The anonymity contract guarantees the user anonymity and message unlinkability so long as she adheres to the contract. Likewise, the service provider is guaranteed to be able to identify users who violate the contract. Attestations convince both the users and service providers that an Accountability Server will enforce precisely the agreed-upon contract. RECAP is interesting because the trusted third party is not biased towards the interests of either the user or the service provider. This bias has been a drawback of many previous anonymity schemes involving a trusted third party.

Saroiu and Wolman [166] and Gilbert et al. [70] propose equipping mobile devices with trusted hardware to attest to the sensor data collected. They argue that many crowd-sourced tasks, such as traffic detection and amateur reporting, would be enhanced by allowing users to demonstrate that sensor readings were not tampered with. Of course, this does not address tampering with the inputs to the sensors themselves.

Finally, researchers have developed schemes with trusted computing building blocks to provide wallet-like functionality for credentials such as passwords, e.g., TruWallet [62].

10 Implementing Trust Bootstrapping: Open Source Tools

Here we introduce a variety of open-source software projects that are highly relevant to bootstrapping trust. At the time of this writing many interesting software packages are available, including a full Linux distribution and several LiveCDs that facilitate experimentation without modifying anything on one's hard drive. These software packages are an excellent starting place for gaining a deeper understanding of the capabilities of existing hardware and software to bootstrap trust.

10.1 Component Packages

First, the Linux kernel has included a device driver for v1.2 TPM chips since v2.6.17. TPM driver support is also included in recent versions of OpenSolaris. Many different TPM drivers exist for Windows, but we are not aware of any open source drivers.

One of the first research projects that endeavored to create a static root of trust was the IBM Integrity Measurement Architecture (IMA) [164], portions of which are available in the default Linux kernel source distribution starting with v2.6.30. Newer kernels are expected to include increasing levels of support.

The TrouSerS project [206] provides much of the supporting infrastructure required to bootstrap trust in a TPM-equipped system, and represents first and foremost an implementation of the TCG Software Stack (TSS). TrouSerS includes the necessary components to bootstrap trust in the Linux kernel's IMA facilities, including the Trusted Grub bootloader that is capable of performing integrity measurements over the kernel before it loads. TrouSerS also includes the `tcsd` daemon (userspace process) that multiplexes access to the system's TPM across multiple applications, and the `libtspi` library against which applications can link to use the TSS API. In addition, TrouSerS provides the `tpm-tools` package to facilitate management of a TPM chip. There is also a `testsuite` that is a valuable resource; it contains many small programs that demonstrate how to exercise specific TPM functionality. Finally, TrouSerS includes an enhanced version of OpenSSL that can leverage TPM-based keys.

jTSS and jTpmTools comprise an alternative TSS and TPM utility library fully written in Java [158, 205]. jTSS communicates directly with the character device `/dev/tpm` that is exposed by the Linux TPM driver. jTpmTools can use jTSS, or it can communicate directly with the TrouSerS TSS.

Two different open-source TPM emulators are available today. Strasser et al. were the first to release one publicly [199], and it has enjoyed experimental integration with several versions of the Xen hypervisor. IBM developed a TPM emulator internally, and eventually released it under an open-source license [74]. Both of these emulators are extremely valuable when developing applications that leverage the TPM, since (by design) it can sometimes be very difficult to debug why a particular TPM operation is failing or otherwise behaving unexpectedly.

Kauer developed the Open Secure Loader (OSLO) shortly after AMD released their first platforms with support for dynamic root of trust (i.e., the *SKINIT* instruction – see Section 5.2) [102]. Intel has released their own reference implementation for their Trusted eXecution Technology (TXT) in the form of the Trusted Boot project [92]. Both `tboot` and OSLO are multiboot-compliant kernels that can subsequently boot Xen or Linux. Prior to booting these other kernels, these modules invoke the *SKINIT* or *GETSEC[SENTER]* instruction to create a dynamic root of trust and perform sanity checks on platform state to ensure a trustworthy boot.

The Flicker project (discussed in Section 5.2) has also released its source code [59]. Flicker is a valuable reference implementation that shows how to invoke a dynamic root of trust for measurement well after a platform boots, thereby bootstrapping trust in a small code module without being burdened by the presence of the legacy operating system code in the trusted computing base for the module of interest. Flicker was initially developed for AMD hardware but has recently been expanded to support both AMD and Intel processors, and to work with both Linux and Windows 7.

The Memoir project [151] (discussed in Section 3.2.2) has also released its source code, building rollback protection on top of the secrecy and integrity protection offered by the Flicker system.

All of these projects offer various ways to ensure that software is measured, or offer developer APIs so that other applications can be written to take advantage of TPM-based functionality. The Open Platform Trust Services (OpenPTS) project [146] takes a wider view; it contains much of the infrastructure required to generate and convey attestations between systems, including protocols and serialized message formats.

10.2 Complete Distributions or LiveCDs

Readers interested in quickly and easily experimenting with the software discussed above may be interested in the Knoppix for Trusted Computing Geeks [108] Linux distribution. The TPM driver, IMA, TrouSerS, Trusted Grub, and other packages are already installed and configured in a LiveCD environment.

The European Open Trusted Computing (OpenTC) project produced the OpenTC Proof of Concept Prototype 1 [147]. This prototype is also in the form of a LiveCD/LiveDVD, and boots the Xen hypervisor and various guest *domains* (Xen terminology for a virtual machine). Sealed storage demonstrations are included.

11 Human Factors & Usability

Most existing work in attestation and trusted computing focuses on interactions between two computing devices. This section treats a higher goal – that of convincing the human operator of a computer that it is in a trustworthy state. These solutions sort into two categories: those where the user is in possession of an additional trustworthy device, and those based solely on the human's sensory and cognitive abilities. An additional, though somewhat orthogonal, category concerns user-friendly techniques to *pair* two trustworthy devices, e.g., to establish a secure channel between two cellphones.

11.1 Trustworthy Verifier Devices

A scientist once gave a public lecture describing how the Earth orbits around the sun and how the sun, in turn, orbits around the center of a collection of stars called our galaxy.

At the end of the lecture, a little old lady at the back of the room got up and said: "What you have told us is rubbish. The world is really a flat plate supported on the back of a giant tortoise."

The scientist gave a superior smile before replying, "What is the tortoise standing on?"

"You're very clever, young man, very clever," said the old lady, "but it's turtles all the way down!"

A user trying to employ one device to verify the trustworthiness of another device quickly realizes that it's "turtles all the way down" because of the endless loop of trust dependencies. Researchers have considered a variety of ways in which to provide the user with one initial turtle (an *iTurtle* [135]) which is axiomatically trustworthy, thereby breaking the dependency loop. This section is dedicated to an extended case study exploring the design space for such a device, including the various research challenges involved.[11]

11.1.1 Overview

Standard remote attestation mechanisms (see Section 4) encounter at least three problems when we adapt them to user-based attestation. All three problems arise because the user does not have an axiomatically trustworthy device to perform verification. (1) The chain of trust created through the verification process does not propagate back to the user, because there is no authenticated channel between the user and the verifier (see Figure 9). (2) In a networked world, it is unclear why the device the user employs as the verifier is any more trustworthy than her other devices. (3) Platform and user privacy are more salient when attestation involves end user machines. We present scenarios to illustrate the above problems.

---

[11] The text in this section is adapted from the work of McCune et al. [135].

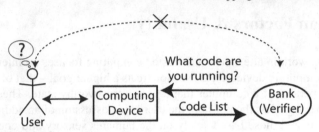

Fig. 9 *Remote attestation does not create an authenticated channel between the verifier and the user. If verification fails, there is no way to inform the user. Thus, malware on the user's computing device can lie about verification results.*

Security-Sensitive Interactive Transactions

Consider a user who wants to perform online banking using her computer. If the bank's server is attestation-aware and the user's computer is attestation-compliant, then the bank's server can request an attestation from the user's computer to verify that the user's computer is running an approved software stack. If the server detects an unapproved software stack, then it can refuse service.

The problem with the above scenario is that there is no way for the bank's server to securely inform the user of the verification result (see Figure 9). If verification is unsuccessful, the user's computer cannot be trusted to display the correct result, since any notification mechanism that displays the verification result on-screen is vulnerable to spoofing. Malware installed on the user's computer could lie to the user that the attestation verified correctly at the bank, display a fake login page, and capture the user's login credentials.

There are two popularly suggested solutions to the problem of establishing an authenticated channel between the user and the bank: side-channels and trusted I/O. Automated side-channels use means of communication other than the user's computer to establish an authenticated channel. For instance, the bank's computer can send SMS messages or make telephone calls to convey the verification result to the user. However, any unauthenticated, automated side-channel may facilitate automated attack. Using a side-channel that is not automated, such as having a customer service representative make a phone call, is also not an option since the attacker can pretend to be a bank employee (a fact amply demonstrated by social engineering attacks). Besides, a non-automated side channel makes the verification expensive and potentially error prone by introducing additional human factors.

Trusted computing technologies, such as AMD's SVM [3] and Intel's Trusted Execution Technology (TXT) [93], which include specification for hardware mechanisms for trusted I/O, do not solve the problem of establishing an authenticated channel between the user and the bank either. While they do include mechanisms for establishing trusted channels between platform components, they do not require any display to indicate that the channel is present [78]. Even if, in the future, these hardware technologies are extended to address this shortcoming, legacy systems will remain a problem.

The online banking example can be extended to any security-sensitive interactive transaction, such as remote login or e-commerce. One may also wish to consider how the problem presented in the above example can be applied to the examples in Chapter 2 of Balacheff et al. [17].

Thus, the best approach may be for the user to use load-time attestation to directly verify her own computer. This would allow the user to trust her computer (to the extent guaranteed by load-time attestation) to correctly display messages sent by the bank.

Specialized Computing Devices

Next, consider specialized computing devices such as 802.11 access points, home routers, GPS navigation systems, and printers. These devices may also contain information or perform tasks that users consider to be security-sensitive (e.g., the integrity of their map data, the secrecy of their printed documents, or the privacy of their photographs), making them attractive targets for malware.

It is unclear how to apply TCG-style remote attestation to these devices, because, in a networked world, the absence of an axiomatically trusted device means that the choice of which device to use as the verifier is not obvious. For example, it is unclear why the user should trust their cell phone to function as a verifier any more than they trust their laptop or desktop computer. Note also that today's attacks have moved "up" the software stack (e.g., cross-site scripting) and may apply to many device types. Furthermore, a third-party remote verifier cannot be used, even if one existed (no such verifiers exist today), since we re-encounter the problem of how to establish an authenticated channel between the user and verifier. Also, the user may not want to employ third-party verifiers due to privacy concerns.

Privacy Issues

During a standard attestation, the verifier learns detailed information about the attestor and the software configuration of the challenged system. As discussed in Section 4.3.2, existing attestation protocols based on the TPM include several privacy-enhancing mechanisms, such as Privacy CAs and Direct Anonymous Attestation. Further, these approaches may hide the identity of the attestor, but not the software configuration of the platform in the attestations. Some of the techniques discussed in Section 5, like property-based attestation, may mitigate the privacy issues created by disclosing software configuration.

However, enabling the user to verify her own computer would alleviate these privacy problems. Further, the user can set privacy policies on her computer with respect to remote attestations and trust the software on her computer to adhere to them (to the extent guaranteed by load-time attestation).

Fig. 10 *Hypothetical scenario showing the use of the iTurtle. On the left, the user learns that her computing device is trustworthy. On the right, the user learns that her computing device has a problem.*

11.1.2 User-Observable Verification

We have discussed ways in which standard attestation fails to provide *user-observable verification*. Here, we explore how one might design a system for user-observable verification, including what some of the desired properties of such a system might be. This will set the stage for Section 11.1.3, where we detail open research issues.

There are two main ways to support device-based user-observable verification: (**1**) Via computing devices that self-verify, or (**2**) Via an inherently trustworthy external device.

Self-verification is not an option on today's computing devices, as we cannot trust a potentially compromised device to report its status correctly. Future architectures may change this. One possibility is to include a trustworthy verification subsystem in every device. However, there is still the problem of how to communicate the result of the verification to the user. One could imagine adding secure I/O capabilities to devices to communicate verification results to the user, although such a design choice may increase the cost and complexity of the trustworthy subsystem. Furthermore, if every manufacturer designs their own user-interface for verification, then the user will be confronted with many different interfaces. This could cause confusion, increase the frequency of mistakes, and degrade user experience, all of which could result in users disregarding the verification process altogether.

Instead of a dedicated verification subsystem inside every device, we could build a single verification device. This alleviates the problem of the user having to learn and use several different verification interfaces. This appears to be the most desirable solution from the point of view of ease of use. This dedicated device provides an unambiguous point from which trust originates for the user. We call this device the *iTurtle*, based on analogy with the "Turtles All the Way Down" story, because it is the turtle on which all other turtles stand, i.e., it is the turtle on which all user trust is built. Figure 10 portrays the iTurtle in use. Assuming a dedicated device is employed, it should support the following properties.

Software Design Simplicity

The software on the iTurtle should be small, since it should be amenable to formal verification or manual audit for security assurance. The software design should avoid the use of cryptographic secrets to eliminate the overhead involved with their maintenance. Such overheads include the use of tamper-resistant or tamper-evident hardware, key management issues like revocation, migration, and regeneration, and vulnerabilities due to lost or stolen iTurtles.

Commodity Hardware

Using commodity hardware will enable inexpensive mass-production of iTurtles. Portions of the software can be borrowed from existing code. Many of the bugs inherent in a new hardware design will have been removed or have known workarounds. A mature developer community will exist to support iTurtle developers.

Universal Physical Connectivity

The iTurtle should use a ubiquitous physical interface. Today, the best choice is likely to be USB. A USB-based iTurtle would have the ability to act as a master or slave device, and would be equipped with adapters for the different USB plug sizes.

Wired Interface

The temptation to use wireless interfaces must be avoided, because without physical connectivity, there is no way (without the use of cryptography) for the human to unambiguously identify the device being verified by the iTurtle. Note that using a wired interface still does not address a relay attack where the challenged machine relays an attestation request to another machine [200].

User Interface Simplicity

The interface which tells the user whether or not verification succeeded should be simple enough to be used by untrained novice users. Simplicity of the user interface should also minimize the opportunities for user error. An example of a simple user interface is a dual-color LED capable of showing a red or a green light, as shown in Figure 10.

Small Form Factor

The iTurtle should be small, lightweight, and rugged. This will enable users to always carry the iTurtle with them, e.g., on a keychain.

11.1.3 Research Issues

A number of research challenges arise when we try to build a verification system using an iTurtle.

What to Verify

Attestation mechanisms verify the software configuration of a computing device, raising the question: *How do we define the software configuration of a computing device?* Below we consider two possible answers, and note their difficulties.

Attestation schemes proposed in the literature treat the software configuration of a computing device as all software that has been loaded for execution since the last reboot [8, 50, 164, 213]. However, even with a small set of installed software, the number of possible software configurations can be large. This is because the number of possible configurations is the number of permutations of the subset of loaded software from the set of all installed software. Some of the problems for the iTurtle include: (1) *How does the iTurtle attach meaning to all of these different configurations?* (2) *How does the iTurtle store so many different configurations for many different devices?*

An alternate scheme would be to define a software configuration as the list of all software that is installed on the device. However, this definition does not take into consideration the problems that arise due to interactions between different software components.

We must also consider the question of how to represent the software configuration of a device, i.e., how to assign identities to software. Another question is how to translate a software configuration into a trust decision.

How to Verify

We now discuss how the iTurtle might verify the software on a computing device, and we identify open research issues. The verification process consists of comparing the software configuration of the device being verified against known-good configurations.

What is a known-good configuration? The user must somehow translate their notion of trust into a set of known-good software configurations. This is a problem with no clear solution. The issue is the semantic gap between a list of program identities and the nebulous notion called trust. The vendor of a computing device might be able to help the users by providing some default known-good configurations for the device.

How does the iTurtle obtain known-good configurations the first time? With trusted computing today, there are at least two possible ways to address this problem. (1) The *Oracle Method* retains a trusted third party as a read-only oracle which provides a list of known-good software configurations to the iTurtle. (2) The *Trusted First Time (TFT) Method* assumes that the system is in a secure state the first time it is verified and compares all subsequent verifications against the first one.

With this verification model, both of these approaches have unresolved issues. Questions which arise with the Oracle Method include: (1) *How does the iTurtle establish an authenticated channel to the oracle?* (2) *How does the user ensure that their privacy is not compromised through oracle queries (i.e., the oracle may be able to infer the software configuration of the user's device if the iTurtle specifically queries the oracle for each piece of software on the user's device)?*

Question (1) does not arise with standard attestation because the verifier is assumed to be a properly configured general-purpose computing device (i.e., it may be assumed to possess authentic public keys), whereas the iTurtle is a special-purpose device with limited capabilities. Standard attestation tries to address question (2) by introducing a layer of indirection between the long-term identity of the user's device and the identity used for oracle queries. This layer of indirection has been realized with techniques such as Privacy CAs [213] or Direct Anonymous Attestation [23]. However, these techniques may be too heavyweight for the iTurtle.

An important question for the TFT Method is: *How does the iTurtle distinguish between a legitimate installation or upgrade and an attack?* The user must somehow convey to the iTurtle that a legitimate upgrade or installation is taking place. Doing this without increasing the complexity of the iTurtle is a challenge.

An additional question for verification is: *How does the user use the same iTurtle to verify multiple devices?* The main issue here is authenticating the device being verified so that the iTurtle uses the correct known-good configuration during verification. Also, interoperability demands a standard protocol for communication between many types of devices and the iTurtle. Standardizing such a protocol is likely to be a significant practical challenge.

What to Do When Verification Fails

Most trusted computing literature does not address procedures for recovering if verification fails, raising the following questions.

How does recovery happen? If the device is compromised, then a trusted entity (the recovery agent) must be involved in recovery. The recovery process may also need to involve the user; however, the level of user expertise required is unclear. It may be necessary to have an expert such as an ISP, a device vendor, or a third party service perform the recovery for a fee. The infrastructure required for involving an expert may be prohibitive.

Where is the recovery agent? The recovery agent can be part of the iTurtle, part of the device, or some combination of both.

If the recovery agent is located on the device, then, for secure recovery, it needs to be isolated from all other software on the device, and the user needs to know that it launched correctly. Technologies such as AMD SVM [3] and Intel TXT [93] provide exactly this functionality, assuming the iTurtle can verify an attestation from the device that a known-good recovery procedure was launched. However, such a system must still authenticate the user's desire to initiate recovery.

If the recovery is performed completely by the iTurtle, then we could design a *Snapping* iTurtle to help revert ("snap") the system state back to a previously known-good state. However, it is unclear how the iTurtle can obtain sufficient control of the device to perform the snap operation without involving any entity on the device. One approach may be to make the iTurtle a bootable device containing a known-good system image. Another approach is to rollback to a known-good state, and then selectively reapply legitimate user actions, but exclude the effects of the malware [72, 106]. The goal is to retain as much of the user's work and data as possible, while still eliminating the malware's effects.

Performing recovery using a combination of the device and the iTurtle might be a practical approach, but additional work is required to discover the details of which operations need to be performed by each of them.

How is recovery initiated? Is it user-invoked or automatic? Both choices have usability issues. User-invoked recovery gives more control to the user but becomes annoying if failure is frequent. Equipping the iTurtle with dedicated hardware to accept the user's recovery request increases its cost and complexity. Automatic recovery removes control from the user, which could also destroy data, interrupt critical work, etc.

Trusting the iTurtle

How can the user trust her iTurtle? Since she cannot directly verify her iTurtle, the only currently available approaches are for the manufacturer of the iTurtle to certify it, or for a trusted third party to certify it. Certification requires standards to be established for the hardware and software components of the iTurtle. If the resulting standard is complex, then certification as well as conformance to standards will be hard. The certification process of TPMs demonstrates this [161].

What if the iTurtle is compromised? We would like to avoid the use of tamper-evident or tamper-resistant hardware, therefore, iTurtle compromise is an issue. The challenges here are: (1) *How does the user detect the compromise?* (2) *When the user detects that her iTurtle is compromised, what should she do?*

Periodic inspection and recertification, and fault tolerant design work well for issues that arise due to normal wear and tear, but they are insufficient to address point (1). For point (2), discarding and replacing the iTurtle is cumbersome, as the user would need to reconfigure the new iTurtle to suit her attestation preferences.

11.1.4 Instantiating an iTurtle

Below, we briefly survey proposals for "iTurtles", i.e., devices that are axiomatically trusted and that can verify other devices.

Some TPM chips include a small number (e.g., fewer than five) of General-Purpose Input/Output (GPIO) pins.[12] These pins are controlled by using the TPM's NVRAM commands with special index values (Section 3.2.2). As access to NVRAM locations can be controlled by PCR values, the same controls are available for GPIO pins. As an example, one could architect a system to illuminate a green LED if an approved hypervisor has been loaded for execution.

To help a human establish trust in a computer, Itoi et al. describe a smart card-based solution called sAEGIS [96]. sAEGIS builds on the AEGIS [8] secure boot architecture (see Section 3.1) but changes the source of the trusted software list. Instead of being preconfigured by a potentially untrustworthy administrator, sAEGIS allows the smart card to serve as the repository of the trusted software list. Thus, a user can insert her smart card into an untrusted computer and reboot. If booting is successful, the resulting environment conforms to the policy encoded on her smart card, i.e., the executing software appears in the list stored on the smart card. Of course, the user must establish through some out-of-band mechanism that the computer indeed employs the sAEGIS system. Otherwise, it might simply ignore the user's smart card.

To help humans verify that a platform is trustworthy, Lee et al. propose the addition of a simple multi-color LED and button to computers to enable interaction with a Trusted Software Module [117]. A complete architecture and implementation for these simple interfaces remains an open problem.

The Zurich Trusted Information Channel (ZTIC) is a USB device designed to serve as a trusted client endpoint for confirming sensitive transactions [220]. It includes a display and several buttons, and it depends on the user's PC only for network communication. The ZTIC is the endpoint of an independent SSL connection to the remote server, and remains secure even if the user's PC is compromised. Although the ZTIC does not attempt to convey any information about the trustworthiness of the user's PC, the user experience of the ZTIC resembles that of the alternatives discussed in this section, and is illustrative for purposes of comparison.

The Bumpy [134] system is an architecture to provide a trusted path for sending input to web pages from a potentially malicious client-side host. A user is assumed to possess a trustworthy smartphone and an encryption-capable keyboard. The smartphone serves as a security indicator to convey the destination for which upcoming input will be encrypted. Users are responsible for prefixing their sensitive input with a secure attention sequence (e.g., @@) and for verifying that the secure attention sequence causes their smartphone to update with the intended destination for the user's forthcoming input. Attestation is used to convince the smartphone that the user's input is being encrypted in an isolated code module.

---

[12] Such pins are an optional portion of the TPM specification.

Libonati et al. present the results of a semester-long user study of the Bumpy system and offer insights for designing security-relevant interfaces and training users to successfully utilize them [122]. For example, they conclude that users appear to readily adapt to employing secure attention sequences (at least generic ones, rather than website-specific ones). Thus, techniques that leverage secure attention sequences to realize useful security properties hold promise. Interactive security indicators appeared to yield better security than ones that a user is asked to simply observe. Even very disruptive and strongly worded warning messages were ignored in multiple cases. This suggests that changing user behavior may require some form of training in which users must redo activities that resulted in insecure actions. Finally, many users appeared to be unprepared to correctly distinguish between *discontinuities* in the user experience caused by benign software updates, and those caused by the malicious actions of an attacker.

As part of an implementation of a red-green system [112] (i.e., a system that partitions a user's applications and activities into an untrusted "red" system and a trusted "green" system), the Lockdown project [215] developed an external USB verifier device with many of the properties discussed in Section 11.1.2.

The Lockdown verifier consists of a single switch, two LEDs, and a buzzer. The switch can be toggled from secure to insecure (or vice versa). Using the TPM's public key, the verifier can authenticate attestations regarding the state of the platform. When the user is in the trusted environment, the green LED is lit. When the user is in the untrusted environment, the red LED is lit. To provide additional feedback to the user (e.g., after she toggles the switch), the verifier uses a blinking red LED to indicate processing. Thus, the user need only remember to check that the green LED is lit before performing security-sensitive tasks. The verifier activates its buzzer to attract the user's attention whenever the LEDs change state. The verifier can also create an alarm buzz if it is unable to verify the correctness of the reference monitor or if the system encounters a fatal error.

The verifier's security display is beyond the control of an adversary and cannot be spoofed or manipulated. Further, the device does not store any secrets or sensitive information and hence does not pose a threat if lost or stolen. Its simple interface (providing essentially one bit of input and one bit of output), makes it easy to understand and use.

11.1.5 Summary

We have discussed the benefits of user-observable verification, surveyed possible instantiations, and highlighted some of the research issues remaining. User-observable verification lends strong privacy properties to trusted computing technologies since the verification process is completely controlled by the user of the computer. Also, users are free to modify and use their computing devices in any way they see fit, even as they do today, while enjoying the security benefits of trusted computing.

11.2 Using Your Brain to Check a Computer

Roots of trust established based on timing measurements (Section 6.4) can potentially be verified by humans. Franklin et al. propose personally verifiable applications as part of the PRISM architecture for human-verifiable code execution [60]. The person inputs a challenge from a physical list and then measures the length of time before the application produces the correct response (also on the list). Verification amounts to checking that the response is correct and that it arrived in a sufficiently short period of time. Such verification relies on the timing-based proposals discussed in Section 6.4.

11.3 Pairing Two Trustworthy Devices

Human factors also come into play when attempting to establish secure communication between two devices, which is often referred to as "pairing". This allows a user, who has successfully bootstrapped trust in two individual devices (using one or more of the techniques we have discussed), to create a secure channel between them. In particular, unlike in earlier discussions, in which one device may be infected with malware, in this setting, the two devices are trusted, and the adversary is assumed to be an external entity.

Proposed pairing strategies include: password entry on one or both device(s) [124, 126]; string comparison that uses the human as a channel to ensure authentic exchange of information [114, 124, 126, 216]; audio-based comparison where the human user compares the strings via audio representation [77, 187]; visual-based comparison of graphics that encode data [54, 156]; shaking devices to create shared entropy pools [33, 88, 119, 128]; common properties of the wireless channel to establish authentic or secret information [30]; and even the electrical conductivity of the human body [188].

There is also research using location-limited channels to exchange keys [18, 31, 133, 145, 193]. The Resurrecting Duckling protocol [193] leverages a direct physical connection between devices for key setup. In the protocol, a mother duck (i.e., the group leader) defines and distributes a key to the ducklings (i.e., the other members of the group). During setup, a policy is uploaded. The policy specifies what actions a duckling will take, (e.g., communicate with other members of the group). Unfortunately, this requires that the mother duck is completely trusted, and the presence of a special interface that supports physical contact.

Talking to Strangers [18] and Capkun's work [31] use demonstrative identification over a location-limited channel (e.g., infrared) to exchange authenticated public keys. Seeing-is-Believing (SiB – recall Section 7.2.3) leverages a digital camera and a 2D barcode displayed electronically as a visual channel to provide demonstrative identification [133, 167]. However, a single SiB exchange provides authentication in one direction only. While a role reversal may be reasonable with smartphones, it is not feasible when one device is a PC or laptop without a camera. Nevertheless, scanning a barcode with a smartphone may be a practical approach to ascertain device identity.

In the realm of access control, researchers have studied a related problem known as the Chess Grandmaster Problem, Mafia Fraud, or Terrorist Fraud [4, 21], in which an adversary acts as a prover to one honest party and a verifier to another party in order to obtain access to a restricted area. Existing solutions rely on distance bounding [21, 22], which, as explained in Section 7.2.1, is ineffective for a TPM, or employ radio-frequency hopping [4] which is also infeasible for most existing hardware roots of trust.

12 Limitations

When it comes to bootstrapping trust in computers, there appear to be significant limitations on the types of guarantees that can be offered against software and hardware attacks. We summarize these limitations below to alert practitioners to the dangers and to inspire more research in these areas.

12.1 Load-Time Versus Run-Time Guarantees

As described in Section 2, existing techniques measure software when it is first loaded. This is the easiest time to obtain a clean snapshot of the program, before, for example, it can create temporary and difficult to inspect local state. However, this approach is fundamentally "brittle", since it leaves open the possibility that malware will exploit the loaded software. For example, if an attacker exploits a buffer overflow in the loaded software, no measurement of this will be recorded. In other words, the information about this platform's state will match that of a platform that contains pristine software. Thus, any vulnerability in the attesting system's software potentially renders the attestation protocol meaningless.

Ideally, we would like a mechanism that provides run-time guarantees, i.e., a mechanism that conveys the *current* state of the platform, rather than information about software loaded on the machine at some arbitrary point in the past. While Sections 2.2 and 5.3 surveyed several attempts to provide run-time properties, they all ultimately depend on a static load-time guarantee. This reinforces the importance of minimizing the amount of software that must be trusted and attested to, since smaller code tends to contain fewer bugs and be more amendable to formal analysis.

12.2 Hardware Attacks

As discussed in Section 6, protection against hardware attacks is typically a tradeoff between cost (and hence ubiquity) and resilience [7]. Below, we discuss some hardware attacks on commodity systems. An important consequence of these attacks is that applications that rely on widespread, commodity secure hardware without physical protections, such as current TPMs, must align the application incentives with those of the person in direct physical control of the platform. Thus, applications that help a user protect her computer from attackers, e.g., an application that verifies the result of an anti-virus scan, are far more likely to succeed than applications such as DRM, which attempt to restrict users' capabilities by keeping secrets from them.

Even simple hardware attacks, such as connecting the TPM's reset pin to ground, can undermine the security offered by this inexpensive solution [102]. Another viable attack is to physically remove the TPM chip and interpose on the Low-Pin Count (LPC) bus that connects the TPM to the chipset. The low speed of the bus makes such interposition feasible and would require less than one thousand dollars in FPGA-based hardware. Tarnovsky shows how to perform a more sophisticated hardware attack [203], but this attack requires costly tools, skills, and equipment including an electron microscope.

This also makes existing TPMs (or similar physically vulnerable devices) a poor choice for kiosk computing. Combining virtualization with a TPM can offer a degree of trust in a kiosk computer [66], but only if the owner of the computer is trusted not to tamper with the TPM itself. Of course, other physical attacks exist, including physical-layer keyboard sniffers and screen-scrapers. The roots of trust we consider in this book are unlikely to ever cope with such attacks.

Similar problems plague cloud computing and electronic voting applications. When a client entrusts a cloud service with sensitive data, it can bootstrap trust in the cloud's software using the techniques we have described, but it cannot verify the security of the cloud's hardware. Thus, the client must trust the cloud provider to deploy adequate physical security. Likewise, a voter might use a trusted device to verify the software on an electronic voting machine, but this information can be undermined by physical attacks on the machine itself. PUFs (Section 6.3) or some of the physical protections discussed in Section 6.1.1 may offer some hope for these settings.

Note, however, that protecting a hardware root of trust may be insufficient. As discussed by many of the references in Section 13.1, the end goal is to create an entire trusted platform, which includes computations performed outside the root of trust, as well as the communication path to and from the user.

For example, hardware attacks on secrets stored in memory can subvert many of the guarantees discussed thus far. Even if a combination of hardware and software protections can protect a user's secrets while the computer is active, recent research by Halderman et al. has shown that data in RAM typically persists for a surprisingly long time (seconds or even minutes) after the computer has been powered down [86]. Hence, an attacker who has physical access to the computer may be able to read these secrets directly out of the computer's memory.

13 Additional Reading

13.1 Books

Trusted Computing Platforms: TCPA Technology in Context

The Trusted Computing Group is actually a successor organization (formed in 2003) to the Trusted Computing Platform Alliance (TCPA). Balacheff et al. document the design of the v1.1b[13] TPM as it emerged from the TCPA era [17]. Note that the v1.1b TPM does not include any support for dynamic root of trust (Section 5.2), and indeed, the only platform change required to support v1.1b was BIOS support for the Core Root of Trust for Measurement (CRTM).

Balacheff et al. discuss the circa 2003 TPM and the TCG Software Stack (TSS) in considerable detail. While today newer resources exist to learn the details of the modern TPM and TSS, Balacheff et al. remains interesting for its extensive set of Usage Scenarios (Chapter 2) and for articulating many of the original motivations for "trusted computing platforms".

Trusted Computing Platforms: Design and Applications

Released in 2005, Smith's book [183] takes a broad perspective and considers the general problem of attempting to establish trust in computation taking place at a remote site, even when the remote system is potentially in the hands of an adversary. Smith discusses a variety of systems, from early work on secure coprocessor design, to the modern Trusted Computing Group efforts, to the contemporary research literature. Both hardware and software attacks are considered.

Smith's role in the design and implementation of the IBM 4758 secure coprocessor is apparent, and the 4758 is the subject of many examples and discussions. The 4758 remains an excellent standard against which to compare other endeavors to realize secure computation. The reader may take interest in the phrase *outbound authentication*, which is a term similar in spirit to, but predating, remote attestation.

Smith's book provides an excellent broad view of the space of general approaches to achieve a "trusted computing platform." Comparatively, the present work is more constrained to the processes involved in bootstrapping trust, and places much less emphasis on maintaining this trust in the face of physically present adversaries.

Trusted Computing

Mitchell's book [140] contains a collection of articles surveying the general field of Trusted Computing as of 2005. It covers the design of Microsoft's now-defunct

---

[13] Two TPM versions enjoy widespread deployment as of the time of this writing: v1.1b, and v1.2.

NGSCB, and it is instructive to see how NGSCB's design influenced hardware developments (e.g., the design of the TPM and of DRTM). Another chapter provides context on the development of DAA, covering the various cryptographic schemes that evolved into the protocol included in the TPM specification. Later chapters examine applications of trusted computing, including topics such as single sign-on, certificate management, digital rights management, certificate management, and peer-to-peer networks. The common theme is the use of attestation to imbue trust in code, and a reliance on isolation, particularly the NGSCB architecture, to allow trusted and untrusted code to coexist.

A Practical Guide to Trusted Computing

While the other books discussed in this section include some practical detail, they are not primarily targeted at developers. In contrast, Challener et al. focus on Trusted Computing from a developer's perspective, providing guidance on writing TPM device drivers or applications that interface with the TCG Software Stack [35]. They also offer advice on porting software applications targeted at the v1.1b version of the TPM and TSS to the v1.2 standard. To the best of our knowledge no widely deployed software leverages these older APIs, although they remain relevant given the deployed base of v1.1b TPM chips. Challener et al. also provide one of the first discussions of dynamic root of trust.

Dynamics of a Trusted Platform

Grawrock covers the motivation and design of the TPM, as well as Intel's dynamic root of trust and virtualization support [79]. Grawrock's book is actually a second edition of sorts, superseding a 2006 book entitled **The Intel Safer Computing Initiative**. Grawrock attempts to motivate the relevant technologies from first principles, and trades off less history of the development of the technology for more detail on Intel-specific technical characteristics. This book contains the most thorough treatment of dynamic root of trust to date.

13.2 Conference and Workshop Proceedings

At least two annual academic conferences exist with a focus on trusted computing, with a significant focus on bootstrapping trust. These are the International Conference on Trust and Trustworthy Computing [207, 208, 209, 210] (in its fourth year as of 2011), and the ACM Scalable Trusted Computing Workshop [194, 195, 196, 197, 198] (in its sixth year as of 2011).

14 Summary

In this book, we organize and clarify extensive research on bootstrapping trust in commodity systems. We identify inconsistencies (e.g., in the types of attacks considered by various forms of secure and trusted boot), and commonalities (e.g., all existing attempts to capture dynamic system properties still rely in some sense on static, load-time guarantees) in previous work. We also consolidate the various types of hardware support available for bootstrapping trust. This leads us to the observation that applications based on low-cost, non-tamper-resistant hardware (e.g., the TPM), must align their incentives with those of the computer owner, suggesting that applications that help the user protect her own secrets or check her computer for malware are more likely to succeed than applications that try to hide information from her. Empirically, users are entrusting increasing amounts of sensitive data and transactions to their computers; we hope the techniques discussed in this book will help enable systems worthy of that trust.

References

All of the URLs listed here are valid as of June, 2011.

[1] Abadi, M., Budiu, M., Erlingsson, U., Ligatti, J.: Control-flow integrity. In: Proceedings of the ACM Conference on Computer and Communications Security (CCS) (2005) (Referenced on page 10.)

[2] Acohido, B., Swartz, J.: Unprotected PCs can be hijacked in minutes. USA Today (2004) (Referenced on page 47.)

[3] Advanced Micro Devices: AMD64 architecture programmer's manual. AMD Publication no. 24593 rev. 3.14 (2007) (Referenced on pages 2, 28, 39, 62, and 68.)

[4] Alkassar, A., Stüble, C., Sadeghi, A.R.: Secure object identification or: Solving the chess grandmaster problem. In: Proceedings of the New Security Paradigm Workshop (NSPW) (2003) (Referenced on page 72.)

[5] Ames Jr, S.R.: Security kernels: A solution or a problem? In: Proceedings of the IEEE Symposium on Security and Privacy (1981) (Referenced on page 25.)

[6] Anderson, R.: Cryptography and competition policy - issues with "Trusted Computing". In: Proceedings of the Workshop on Economics and Information Security (2003) (Referenced on page 1.)

[7] Anderson, R., Kuhn, M.: Tamper resistance – a cautionary note. In: Proceedings of the USENIX Workshop on Electronic Commerce (1995) (Referenced on page 73.)

[8] Arbaugh, W.A., Farber, D.J., Smith, J.M.: A reliable bootstrap architecture. In: Proceedings of the IEEE Symposium on Security and Privacy, pp. 65–71 (1997) (Referenced on pages 13, 36, 66, and 69.)

[9] ARM: ARM security technology. PRD29-GENC-009492C (2009) (Referenced on pages 1 and 38.)

[10] Armknecht, F., Maes, R., Sadeghi, A.R., Standaert, F.X., Wachsmann, C.: A formal foundation for the security features of physical functions. In: IEEE Symposium on Security and Privacy (2011) (Referenced on page 39.)

[11] Arnold, T., van Doorn, L.: The IBM PCIXCC: A new cryptographic coprocessor for the IBM eServer. IBM Journal of Research and Development **48**(3) (2004) (Referenced on page 35.)

[12] Azab, A.M., Ning, P., Wang, Z., Jiang, X., Zhang, X., Skalsky, N.C.: HyperSentry: Enabling stealthy in-context measurement of hypervisor integrity. In: Proceedings of the ACM Conference on Computer and Communications Security (CCS) (2010) (Referenced on page 27.)

[13] Azema, J., Fayad, G.: M-Shield mobile security technology: making wireless secure. Texas Instruments Whitepaper. Available at `http://focus.ti.com/pdfs/wtbu/ti_mshield_whitepaper.pdf` (2008) (Referenced on pages 1 and 38.)

[14] Baek, K.H., Smith., S.: Preventing theft of quality of service on open platforms. In: Proceedings of the IEEE/CREATE-NET Workshop on Security and QoS in Communication Networks (2005) (Referenced on page 55.)

[15] Baiardi, F., Cilea, D., Sgandurra, D., Ceccarelli, F.: Measuring semantic integrity for remote attestation. In: Proceedings of the International Conference on Trusted Computing (2009) (Referenced on page 10.)

[16] Bailey, K.A., Smith, S.W.: Trusted virtual containers on demand. In: Proceedings of the ACM Workshop on Scalable Trusted Computing (STC) (2010) (Referenced on page 5.)

[17] Balacheff, B., Chen, L., Pearson, S., Plaquin, D., Proudler, G.: Trusted Computing Platforms – TCPA Technology in Context. Prentice Hall (2003) (Referenced on pages 63 and 75.)

[18] Balfanz, D., Smetters, D., Stewart, P., Wong, H.C.: Talking to strangers: Authentication in ad-hoc wireless networks. In: Proceedings of the ISOC Symposium on Network and Distributed System Security (NDSS) (2002) (Referenced on page 71.)

[19] Belenkiy, M., Chase, M., Erway, C.C., Jannotti, J., Küpçü, A., Lysyanskaya, A.: Incentivizing outsourced computation. In: Proceedings of the Workshop on Economics of Networked Systems (NetEcon) (2008) (Referenced on page 40.)

[20] Berger, S., Cáceres, R., Goldman, K.A., Perez, R., Sailer, R., van Doorn, L.: vTPM: Virtualizing the trusted platform module. In: Proceedings of the USENIX Security Symposium (2006) (Referenced on page 5.)

[21] Beth, T., Desmedt, Y.: Identification tokens - or: Solving the chess grandmaster problem. In: Proceedings of CRYPTO (1991) (Referenced on page 72.)

[22] Brands, S., Chaum, D.: Distance-bounding protocols. In: Proceedings of EuroCrypt (1994) (Referenced on pages 46 and 72.)

[23] Brickell, E., Camenisch, J., Chen, L.: Direct anonymous attestation. In: Proceedings of the ACM Conference on Computer and Communications Security (CCS) (2004) (Referenced on pages 23 and 67.)

[24] Brickell, E., Li, J.: A pairing-based DAA scheme further reducing TPM resources. In: Proceedings of the International Conference on Trust and Trustworthy Computing (2010) (Referenced on page 24.)

[25] Brumley, D., Song, D.: Privtrans: Automatically partitioning programs for privilege separation. In: Proceedings of the USENIX Security Symposium (2004) (Referenced on page 31.)

[26] Bruschi, D., Cavallaro, L., Lanzi, A., Monga, M.: Replay attack in TCG specification and solution. In: Proceedings of the Annual Computer Security Applications Conference (ACSAC) (2005) (Referenced on page 51.)

[27] Bugiel, S., Ekberg, J.E.: Implementing an application-specific credential platform using late-launched mobile trusted module. In: Proceedings of the ACM Workshop on Scalable Trusted Computing (STC) (2010) (Referenced on page 38.)

[28] Busch, H., Sotáková, M., Katzenbeisser, S., Sion, R.: The PUF promise. In: Proceedings of the International Conference on Trust and Trustworthy Computing (2010) (Referenced on page 39.)

[29] Bussani, A., Griffin, J.L., Jansen, B., Julisch, K., Karjoth, G., Maruyama, H., Nakamura, M., Perez, R., Schunter, M., Tanner, A., Van Doorn, L., Van Herreweghen, E.A., Waidner, M., Yoshihama, S.: Trusted Virtual Domains: Secure foundations for business and IT services. Tech. Rep. RC23792, IBM Research (2005) (Referenced on page 5.)

[30] Cagalj, M., Capkun, S., Hubaux, J.P.: Key agreement in peer-to-peer wireless networks. Proceedings of the IEEE (Special Issue on Cryptography) **94**, 467–478 (2006) (Referenced on page 71.)

[31] Capkun, S., Hubaux, J.P., Buttyan, L.: Mobility helps security in ad hoc networks. In: Proceedings of the ACM Symposium on Mobile Ad Hoc Networking & Computing (MobiHoc) (2003) (Referenced on page 71.)

[32] Castelluccia, C., Francillon, A., Perito, D., Soriente, C.: On the difficulty of software-based attestation of embedded devices. In: Proceedings of the ACM Conference on Computer and Communications Security (CCS) (2009) (Referenced on page 40.)

[33] Castelluccia, C., Mutaf, P.: Shake them up! A movement-based pairing protocol for CPU-constrained devices. In: Proceeding of the Conference on Mobile Systems, Applications, and Services (MobiSys) (2005) (Referenced on page 71.)

[34] Catuogno, L., Dmitrienko, A., Eriksson, K., Kuhlmann, D., Ramunno, G., Sadeghi, A.R., Schulz, S., Schunter, M., Winandy, M., Zhan, J.: Trusted virtual domains - design, implementation and lessons learned. In: Proceedings of the International Conference on Trusted Systems (INTRUST) (2009) (Referenced on page 5.)

[35] Challener, D., Hoff, J., Catherman, R., Safford, D., van Doorn, L.: Practical Guide to Trusted Computing. Prentice Hall (2007) (Referenced on page 76.)

[36] Chen, B., Morris, R.: Certifying program execution with secure procesors. In: Proceedings of the USENIX Workshop on Hot Topics in Operating Systems (HotOS) (2003) (Referenced on page 36.)

[37] Chen, L.: A DAA scheme using batch proof and verification. In: Proceedings of the International Conference on Trust and Trustworthy Computing (2010) (Referenced on page 24.)

[38] Chen, L., Landfermann, R., Löhr, H., Rohe, M., Sadeghi, A.R., Stüble, C.: A protocol for property-based attestation. In: Proceedings of the ACM Workshop on Scalable Trusted Computing (STC) (2006) (Referenced on page 33.)

[39] Chen, L., Ryan, M.D.: Offline dictionary attack on TCG TPM weak authorisation data, and solution. In: Proceedings of the Conference on Future of Trust in Computing (2008) (Referenced on page 51.)

[40] Chen, S., Xu, J., Sezer, E.C., Gauriar, P., Iyer, R.K.: Non-control-data attacks are realistic threats. In: Proceedings of the USENIX Security Symposium (2005) (Referenced on page 10.)

[41] Chen, X., Garfinkel, T., Lewis, E.C., Subrahmanyam, P., Waldspurger, C.A., Boneh, D., Dwoskin, J., Ports, D.R.K.: Overshadow: A virtualization-based approach to retrofitting protection in commodity operating systems. In: Proceedings of the ACM Conference on Architectural Support for Programming Languages and Operating Systems (ASPLOS) (2008) (Referenced on page 27.)

[42] Chen, Y., England, P., Peinado, M., Willman, B.: High assurance computing on open hardware architectures. Tech. Rep. MSR-TR-2003-20, Microsoft Research (2003) (Referenced on page 26.)

[43] Chun, B.G., Maniatis, P., Shenker, S., Kubiatowicz, J.: Attested append-only memory: Making adversaries stick to their word. In: Proceedings of the ACM Symposium on Operating Systems Principles (SOSP) (2007) (Referenced on page 39.)

[44] Clark, D.D., Wilson, D.R.: A comparison of commercial and military security policies. In: Proceedings of the IEEE Symposium on Security and Privacy (1987) (Referenced on page 26.)

[45] Coker, G., Guttman, J., Loscocco, P., Herzog, A., Millen, J., O'Hanlon, B., Ramsdell, J., Segall, A., Sheehy, J., Sniffen, B.: Principles of remote attestation. International Journal of Information Security 10(2) (2011) (Referenced on page 21.)

[46] Datta, A., Franklin, J., Garg, D., Kaynar, D.: A logic of secure systems and its application to trusted computing. In: Proceedings of the IEEE Symposium on Security and Privacy (2009) (Referenced on page 52.)

[47] Dietrich, K., Winter, J.: Towards customizable, application specific mobile trusted modules. In: Proceedings of the ACM Workshop on Scalable Trusted Computing (STC) (2010) (Referenced on page 38.)

[48] Dixon, C., Uppal, H., Brajkovic, V., Brandon, D., Anderson, T., Krishnamurthy, A.: ETTM: A scalable fault tolerant network manager. In: Proceedings of the USENIX Symposium on Networked Systems Design and Implementation (NSDI) (2011) (Referenced on page 56.)

[49] Dwoskin, J.S., Gomathisankaran, M., Chen, Y.Y., Lee, R.B.: A framework for testing hardware-software security architectures. In: Proceedings of the Annual Computer Security Applications Conference (ACSAC) (2010) (Referenced on page 51.)

[50] Dyer, J., Lindemann, M., Perez, R., Sailer, R., van Doorn, L., Smith, S.W., Weingart, S.: Building the IBM 4758 Secure Coprocessor. IEEE Computer (2001) (Referenced on pages 14 and 66.)

[51] Einstein, A.: On the electrodynamics of moving bodies. Annalen der Physik 17, 891–921 (1905) (Referenced on page 46.)

[52] Ekberg, J.E., Bugiel, S.: Trust in a small package: minimized MRTM software implementation for mobile secure environments. In: Proceedings of the ACM Workshop on Scalable Trusted Computing (STC) (2009) (Referenced on page 38.)

[53] Ekberg, J.E., Kylänpää, M.: Mobile trusted module (MTM) - an introduction. Tech. Rep. NRC-TR-2007-015, Nokia Research Center (2007) (Referenced on pages 37, 38, and 54.)

[54] Ellison, C., Dohrmann, S.: Public-key support for group collaboration. ACM Transactions on Information and System Security **6**(4) (2003) (Referenced on page 71.)

[55] England, P., Lampson, B., Manferdelli, J., Peinado, M., Willman, B.: A trusted open platform. IEEE Computer **36**(7), 55–62 (2003) (Referenced on page 26.)

[56] Erlingsson, U., Abadi, M., Vrable, M., Budiu, M., Necula, G.C.: XFI: Software guards for system address spaces. In: Proceedings of the USENIX Symposium on Operating Systems Design and Implementation (OSDI) (2006) (Referenced on pages 10 and 32.)

[57] Feng, W.C., Schluessler, T.: The case for network witnesses. In: Proceedings of the IEEE Workshop on Secure Network Protocols (2008) (Referenced on page 56.)

[58] Finney, H.: PrivacyCA. http://privacyca.com (Referenced on page 23.)

[59] Flicker: Minimal TCB code execution. Source code v0.5: http://flickertcb.sourceforge.net/ (Referenced on page 60.)

[60] Franklin, J., Luk, M., Seshadri, A., Perrig, A.: PRISM: Enabling personal verification of code integrity, untampered execution, and trusted I/O or human-verifiable code execution. Tech. Rep. CMU-CyLab-07-010, Carnegie Mellon University, Cylab (2007) (Referenced on page 71.)

[61] Fujisaki, E., Okamoto, T., Pointcheval, D., Stern, J.: RSA–OAEP is secure under the RSA assumption. In: Proceedings of CRYPTO (2001) (Referenced on page 15.)

[62] Gajek, S., Löhr, H., Sadeghi, A.R., Winandy, M.: TruWallet: trustworthy and migratable wallet-based web authentication. In: Proceedings of the ACM Workshop on Scalable Trusted Computing (STC) (2009) (Referenced on page 57.)

[63] Gallo, R., Kawakami, H., Dahab, R., Arajo, G., Azavedo, R.: T-DRE: A hardware trusted computing base for direct recording electronic vote machines. In: Proceedings of the Annual Computer Security Applications Conference (ACSAC) (2010) (Referenced on page 54.)

[64] Garfinkel, T., Pfaff, B., Chow, J., Rosenblum, M., Boneh, D.: Terra: A virtual machine-based platform for trusted computing. In: Proceedings of the Symposium on Operating System Principles (SOSP) (2003) (Referenced on pages 5, 6, 7, 21, 27, and 32.)

[65] Garfinkel, T., Rosenblum, M., Boneh, D.: Flexible OS support and applications for Trusted Computing. In: Proceedings of the USENIX Workshop on Hot Topics in Operating Systems (HotOS) (2003) (Referenced on page 55.)

[66] Garriss, S., Cáceres, R., Berger, S., Sailer, R., van Doorn, L., Zhang, X.: Trustworthy and personalized computing on public kiosks. In: Proceedings of the Conference on Mobile Systems, Applications, and Services (MobiSys) (2008) (Referenced on pages 49 and 74.)

[67] Gasmi, Y., Sadeghi, A.R., Stewin, P., Unger, M., Winandy, M., Husseiki, R., Stüble, C.: Flexible and secure enterprise rights management based on trusted virtual domains. In: Proceedings of the ACM Workshop on Scalable Trusted Computing (STC) (2008) (Referenced on page 5.)

[68] Gasser, M., Goldstein, A., Kaufman, C., Lampson, B.: The digital distributed system security architecture. In: Proceedings of the National Computer Security Conference (1989) (Referenced on pages 1, 4, 5, 6, 7, and 13.)

[69] Giffin, J.T., Christodorescu, M., Kruger, L.: Strengthening software self-checksumming via self-modifying code. In: Proceedings of the Annual Computer Security Applications Conference (ACSAC) (2005) (Referenced on pages 39 and 40.)

[70] Gilbert, P., Cox, L.P., Jung, J., Wetherall, D.: Toward trustworthy mobile sensing. In: Proceedings of the ACM Workshop on Mobile Computing Systems and Applications (HotMobile) (2010) (Referenced on page 57.)

[71] Gobioff, H., Smith, S., Tygar, J., Yee, B.: Smart cards in hostile environments. In: Proceedings of the USENIX Workshop on Electronic Commerce (1995) (Referenced on page 36.)

[72] Goel, A., Po, K., Farhadi, K., Li, Z., de Lara, E.: The taser intrusion recovery system. In: Proceedings of the ACM Symposium on Operating Systems Principles (SOSP) (2005) (Referenced on page 68.)

[73] Gold, B.D., Linde, R.R., Cudney, P.F.: KVM/370 in retrospect. In: Proceedings of the IEEE Symposium on Security and Privacy (1984) (Referenced on page 25.)

[74] Goldman, K.: IBM's software Trusted Platform Module. Source code: http://ibmswtpm.sourceforge.net/ (Referenced on page 59.)

[75] Goldman, K., Perez, R., Sailer, R.: Linking remote attestation to secure tunnel endpoints. In: Proceedings of the ACM Workshop on Scalable Trusted Computing (STC) (2006) (Referenced on pages 21 and 22.)

[76] Goldman, K., Sailer, R., Pendarakis, D., Srinivasan, D.: Scalable integrity monitoring in virtualized environments. In: Proceedings of the ACM Workshop on Scalable Trusted Computing (STC) (2010) (Referenced on page 6.)

[77] Goodrich, M.T., Sirivianos, M., Solis, J., Tsudik, G., Uzun, E.: Loud and clear: Human-verifiable authentication based on audio. In: Proceedings of the IEEE International Conference on Distributed Computing Systems (ICDCS) (2006) (Referenced on page 71.)

[78] Grawrock, D.: The Intel Safer Computing Initiative: Building Blocks for Trusted Computing. Intel Press (2006) (Referenced on page 62.)

[79] Grawrock, D.: Dynamics of a Trusted Platform. Intel Press (2008) (Referenced on page 76.)

[80] GSM Association: GSM mobile phone technology adds another billion connections in just 30 months. GSM World Press Release (2006) (Referenced on page 1.)

[81] Gueron, S., Kounavis, M.E.: New processor instructions for accelerating encryption and authentication algorithms. Intel Technology Journal 13(2) (2009) (Referenced on page 2.)

[82] Gummadi, R., Balakrishnan, H., Maniatis, P., Ratnasamy, S.: Not-a-bot: Improving service availability in the face of botnet attacks. In: Proceedings of the USENIX Symposium on Networked Systems Design and Implementation (NSDI) (2009) (Referenced on page 56.)

[83] Gürgens, S., Rudolph, C., Scheuermann, D., Atts, M., Plaga, R.: Security evaluation of scenarios based on the TCG's TPM specification. In: Proceedings of the European Symposium on Research in Computer Security (ESORICS) (2007) (Referenced on page 51.)

[84] Haeberlen, A., Aditya, P., Rodrigues, R., Druschel, P.: Accountable virtual machines. In: Proceedings of the USENIX Symposium on Operating Systems Design and Implementation (OSDI) (2010) (Referenced on page 40.)

[85] Haldar, V., Chandra, D., Franz, M.: Semantic remote attestation: a virtual machine directed approach to trusted computing. In: Proceedings of the Conference on Virtual Machine Research (2004) (Referenced on pages 10, 25, 32, and 33.)

[86] Halderman, J.A., Schoen, S.D., Heninger, N., Clarkson, W., Paul, W., Calandrino, J.A., Feldman, A.J., Appelbaum, J., Felten, E.W.: Lest we remember: Cold boot attacks on encryption keys. In: Proceedings of the USENIX Security Symposium (2008) (Referenced on page 74.)

[87] von Helden, J., Bente, I., Vieweg, J.: Trusted Network Connect (TNC). European Trusted Infrastructure Summer School (2009) (Referenced on page 54.)

[88] Holmquist, L.E., Mattern, F., Schiele, B., Alahuhta, P., Beigl, M., Gellersen, H.W.: Smart-its friends: A technique for users to easily establish connections between smart artefacts. In: Proceedings of the ACM Conference on Ubiquitous Computing (Ubicomp) (2001) (Referenced on page 71.)

[89] IBM: CCA basic services reference and guide for the IBM 4758 PCI and IBM 4764 PCI-X cryptographic coprocessors. 19th Ed. (2008) (Referenced on page 35.)

[90] Infineon Technologies AG: Infineon chip card and security ICs portfolio. http://www.infineon.com (2010) (Referenced on page 36.)

[91] Intel, HP, NEC, Dell: IPMI - Intelligent Platform Management Interface specification second generation v2.0. http://download.intel.com/design/servers/ipmi/IPMIv2_0rev1_0.pdf (2004) (Referenced on page 27.)

[92] Intel Corporation: Trusted boot. Source code: http://tboot.sourceforge.net/ (Referenced on page 60.)

[93] Intel Corporation: Intel trusted execution technology – measured launched environment developer's guide. Document number 315168-005 (2008) (Referenced on pages 2, 28, 29, 39, 62, and 68.)

[94] Intel Corporation: Intel vPro Technology. http://www.intel.com/ technology/vpro/ (2011) (Referenced on page 27.)

[95] Itoi, N.: Secure coprocessor integration with Kerberos V5. In: Proceedings of the USENIX Security Symposium (2000) (Referenced on page 55.)

[96] Itoi, N., Arbaugh, W.A., Pollack, S.J., Reeves, D.M.: Personal secure booting. In: Proceedings of the Australasian Conference on Information Security and Privacy (ACISP) (2000) (Referenced on page 69.)

[97] Jaeger, T., Sailer, R., Shankar, U.: PRIMA: policy-reduced integrity measurement architecture. In: Proceedings of the ACM Symposium on Access Control Models And Technologies (SACMAT) (2006) (Referenced on page 26.)

[98] Jiang, S.: WebALPS implementation and performance analysis. Master's thesis, Dartmouth College (2001) (Referenced on page 55.)

[99] Jiang, S., Smith, S., Minami, K.: Securing web servers against insider attack. In: Proceedings of the Annual Computer Security Applications Conference (ACSAC) (2001) (Referenced on pages 14 and 35.)

[100] Johnson, R., Wagner, D.: Finding user/kernel pointer bugs with type inference. In: Proceedings of the USENIX Security Symposium (2004) (Referenced on page 32.)

[101] Karger, P.A., Zurko, M.E., Bonin, D.W., Mason, A.H., Kahn, C.E.: A retrospective on the VAX VMM security kernel. IEEE Transactions on Software Engineering 17(11), 1147–1165 (1991) (Referenced on page 25.)

[102] Kauer, B.: OSLO: Improving the security of Trusted Computing. In: Proceedings of the USENIX Security Symposium (2007). Source code: http://os.inf.tu-dresden.de/~kauer/oslo/ (Referenced on pages 21, 30, 51, 60, and 73.)

[103] Keller, E., Lee, R.B., Rexford, J.: Accountability in hosted virtual networks. In: Proceedings of the ACM Workshop on Virtualized Infrastructure Systems and Architectures (VISA) (2009) (Referenced on page 55.)

[104] Kennell, R., Jamieson, L.: Establishing the genuinity of remote computer systems. In: Proceedings of the USENIX Security Symposium (2003) (Referenced on pages 39 and 40.)

[105] Kil, C., Sezer, E.C., Azab, A., Ning, P., Zhang, X.: Remote attestation to dynamic system properties. In: Proceedings of the IEEE/IFIP Conference on Dependable Systems and Networks (DSN) (2009) (Referenced on pages 10 and 32.)

[106] Kim, T., Wang, X., Zeldovich, N., Kaashoek, M.F.: Intrusion recovery using selective re-execution. In: Proceedings of the USENIX Symposium on Operating Systems Design and Implementation (OSDI) (2010) (Referenced on page 68.)

[107] Klein, G., Elphinstone, K., Heiser, G., Andronick, J., Cock, D., Derrin, P., Elkaduwe, D., Engelhardt, K., Norrish, M., Kolanski, R., Sewell, T., Tuch,

H., Winwood, S.: seL4: Formal verification of an OS kernel. In: Proceedings of the ACM Symposium on Operating Systems Principles (SOSP) (2009) (Referenced on page 25.)

[108] Knoppix for trusted computing geeks. http://unit.aist.go.jp/itri/knoppix/index-en.html (Referenced on page 60.)

[109] Korthaus, R., Sadeghi, A.R., Stüble, C., Zhan, J.: A practical property-based bootstrap architecture. In: Proceedings of the ACM Workshop on Scalable Trusted Computing (STC) (2009) (Referenced on page 33.)

[110] Krautheim, F.J., Phatak, D.S., Sherman, A.T.: Introducing the trusted virtual environment module: A new mechanism for rooting trust in cloud computing. In: Proceedings of the International Conference on Trust and Trustworthy Computing (2010) (Referenced on page 6.)

[111] Kühn, U., Selhorst, M., Stüble, C.: Realizing property-based attestation and sealing with commonly available hard- and software. In: Proceedings of the ACM Workshop on Scalable Trusted Computing (STC) (2007) (Referenced on page 33.)

[112] Lampson, B.: Usable security: How to get it. Communications of the ACM 52(11) (2009) (Referenced on page 70.)

[113] Lang, P.: Flash the Intel BIOS with confidence. Intel Developer UPDATE Magazine (2002) (Referenced on page 50.)

[114] Laur, S., Nyberg, K.: Efficient mutual data authentication using manually authenticated strings. In: Proceedings of the Conference on Cryptology and Network Security (CANS) (2006) (Referenced on page 71.)

[115] LeClaire, J.: Apple ships iPods with Windows virus. Mac News World (2006) (Referenced on page 47.)

[116] Lee, D., Wester, B., Veeraraghavan, K., Narayanasamy, S., Chen, P.M., Flinn, J.: Respec: Efficient online multiprocessor replay via speculation and external determinism. In: Proceedings of the ACM Conference on Architectural Support for Programming Languages and Operating Systems (ASPLOS) (2010) (Referenced on page 40.)

[117] Lee, R.B., Kwan, P., McGregor, J.P., Dwoskin, J., Wang, Z.: Architecture for protecting critical secrets in microprocessors. In: Proceedings of the International Symposium on Computer Architecture (ISCA) (2005) (Referenced on pages 36, 51, and 69.)

[118] van der Leest, V., Schrijen, G.J., Handschuh, H., Tuyls, P.: Hardware intrinsic security from D flip-flops. In: Proceedings of the ACM Workshop on Scalable Trusted Computing (STC) (2010) (Referenced on page 39.)

[119] Lester, J., Hannaford, B., Gaetano, B.: Are you with me? - Using accelerometers to determine if two devices are carried by the same person. In: Proceedings of Pervasive (2004) (Referenced on page 71.)

[120] Leung, A., Chen, L., Mitchell, C.J.: On a possible privacy flaw in direct anonymous attestation (DAA). In: Proceedings of the International Conference on Trusted Computing (2008) (Referenced on page 24.)

[121] Levin, D., Douceur, J.R., Lorch, J.R., Moscibroda, T.: TrInc: Small trusted hardware for large distributed systems. In: Proceedings of the USENIX Sym-

posium on Networked Systems Design and Implementation (NSDI) (2009) (Referenced on page 39.)

[122] Libonati, A., McCune, J.M., Reiter, M.K.: Usability testing a malware-resistant input mechanism. In: Proceedings of the ISOC Symposium on Network and Distributed Systems Security (NDSS) (2011) (Referenced on page 70.)

[123] Lie, D., Thekkath, C.A., Mitchell, M., Lincoln, P., Boneh, D., Mitchell, J.C., Horowitz, M.: Architectural support for copy and tamper resistant software. In: Proceedings of the ACM Conference on Architectural Support for Programming Languages and Operating Systems (ASPLOS) (2000) (Referenced on page 36.)

[124] Linksky, J. et al.: Simple Pairing Whitepaper, revision v10r00. http://mclean-linsky.net/joel/cv/Simple%20Pairing_WP_V10r00.pdf (2006) (Referenced on page 71.)

[125] Löhr, H., Pöppelmann, T., Rave, J., Steegmanns, M., Winandy, M.: Trusted virtual domains on OpenSolaris: usable secure desktop environments. In: Proceedings of the ACM Workshop on Scalable Trusted Computing (STC) (2010) (Referenced on page 5.)

[126] Lortz, V., Roberts, D., Erdmann, B., Dawidowsky, F., Hayes, K., Yee, J.C., Ishidoshiro, T.: Wi-Fi Simple Config Specification, version 1.0a (2006). Now known as Wi-Fi Protected Setup (Referenced on page 71.)

[127] Marchesini, J., Smith, S.W., Wild, O., Stabiner, J., Barsamian, A.: Open-source applications of TCPA hardware. In: Proceedings of the Annual Computer Security Applications Conference (ACSAC) (2004) (Referenced on pages 4, 8, 21, and 25.)

[128] Mayrhofer, R., Gellersen, H.: Shake well before use: Intuitive and secure pairing of mobile devices. IEEE Transactions on Mobile Computing 8(6) (2009) (Referenced on page 71.)

[129] McCune, J.M., Li, Y., Qu, N., Zhou, Z., Datta, A., Gligor, V., Perrig, A.: TrustVisor: Efficient TCB reduction and attestation. In: Proceedings of the IEEE Symposium on Security and Privacy (2010) (Referenced on page 30.)

[130] McCune, J.M., Parno, B., Perrig, A., Reiter, M.K., Isozaki, H.: Flicker: An execution infrastructure for TCB minimization. In: Proceedings of the ACM European Conference on Computer Systems (EuroSys) (2008) (Referenced on pages 21, 22, 30, and 55.)

[131] McCune, J.M., Parno, B., Perrig, A., Reiter, M.K., Seshadri, A.: Minimal TCB code execution (extended abstract). In: Proceedings of the IEEE Symposium on Security and Privacy (2007) (Referenced on pages 22 and 30.)

[132] McCune, J.M., Parno, B., Perrig, A., Reiter, M.K., Seshadri, A.: How low can you go? Recommendations for hardware-supported minimal TCB code execution. In: Proceedings of the ACM Conference on Architectural Support for Programming Languages and Operating Systems (ASPLOS) (2008) (Referenced on pages 30 and 46.)

[133] McCune, J.M., Perrig, A., Reiter, M.K.: Seeing-is-believing: Using camera phones for human-verifiable authentication. In: Proceedings of the IEEE Symposium on Security and Privacy (2005) (Referenced on pages 49 and 71.)

[134] McCune, J.M., Perrig, A., Reiter, M.K.: Safe passage for passwords and other sensitive data. In: Proceedings of the ISOC Symposium on Network and Distributed System Security (NDSS) (2009) (Referenced on page 69.)

[135] McCune, J.M., Perrig, A., Seshadri, A., van Doorn, L.: Turtles all the way down: Research challenges in user-based attestation. In: Proceedings of the USENIX Workshop on Hot Topics in Security (HotSec) (2007) (Referenced on page 61.)

[136] Merkle, R.C.: A certified digital signature. In: Proceedings of CRYPTO (1989) (Referenced on page 56.)

[137] Microsoft Corporation: Code access security. MSDN .NET Framework Developer's Guide – Visual Studio .NET Framework 3.5 (2008) (Referenced on page 53.)

[138] Microsoft Corporation: Full volume encryption using Windows BitLocker drive encryption. Microsoft Services Datasheet (2008) (Referenced on page 53.)

[139] Millen, J., Guttman, J., Ramsdell, J., Sheehy, J., Sniffen, B.: Analysis of a measured launch. Tech. Rep. 07-0843, The MITRE Corporation (2007) (Referenced on page 51.)

[140] Mitchell, C. (ed.): Trusted Computing. The Institution of Electrical Engineers (2005) (Referenced on pages 26 and 75.)

[141] Monate, B., Signoles, J.: Slicing for security of code. In: Proceedings of the International Conference on Trust and Trustworthy Computing (2008) (Referenced on page 32.)

[142] Monrose, F., Wyckoff, P., Rubin, A.: Distributed execution with remote audit. In: Proceedings of ISOC Network and Distributed System Security Symposium (NDSS) (1999) (Referenced on page 40.)

[143] Moyer, T., Butler, K., Schiffman, J., McDaniel, P., Jaeger, T.: Scalable web content attestation. In: Proceedings of the Annual Computer Security Applications Conference (ACSAC) (2009) (Referenced on page 55.)

[144] Nauman, M., Alam, M., Zhang, X., Ali, T.: Remote attestation of attribute updates and information flows in a UCON system. In: Proceedings of the International Conference on Trusted Computing (2009) (Referenced on page 32.)

[145] NFC Forum: Specifications. http://www.nfc-forum.org/specs/ (Referenced on page 71.)

[146] Open platform trust services (OpenPTS). Source code: http://openpts.sourceforge.jp (Referenced on page 60.)

[147] OpenTC proof of concept prototype 1. http://www.opentc.net/index.php?option=com_content&task=view&id=45&Itemid=63 (Referenced on page 60.)

[148] Pappu, R., Recht, B., Taylor, J., Gershenfeld, N.: Physical one-way functions. Science **297**(5589) (2002) (Referenced on page 39.)

[149] Parno, B.: Bootstrapping trust in a "trusted" platform. In: Proceedings of the USENIX Workshop on Hot Topics in Security (HotSec) (2008) (Referenced on page 41.)

[150] Parno, B.: Trust extension as a mechanism for secure code execution on commodity computers. Ph.D. thesis, Carnegie Mellon University (2010) (Referenced on page 56.)

[151] Parno, B., Lorch, J.R., Douceur, J.R., Mickens, J., McCune, J.M.: Memoir: Practical state continuity for protected modules. In: Proceedings of the IEEE Symposium on Security and Privacy (2011). Source code: http://research.microsoft.com/en-us/projects/memoir/ (Referenced on pages 17 and 60.)

[152] Parno, B., McCune, J.M., Perrig, A.: Bootstrapping trust in commodity computers. In: Proceedings of the IEEE Symposium on Security and Privacy (2010) (Referenced on page vii.)

[153] Parno, B., Zhou, Z., Perrig, A.: Help me help you: Using trustworthy host-based information in the network. Tech. Rep. CMU-CyLab-09-016, Carnegie Mellon University, Cylab (2009) (Referenced on page 56.)

[154] Perrig, A., van Doorn, L.: Refutation of "On the difficulty of software-based attestation of embedded devices". http://sparrow.ece.cmu.edu/group/pub/perrig-vandoorn-refutation.pdf (2010) (Referenced on page 40.)

[155] Perrig, A., Smith, S., Song, D., Tygar, J.: SAM: A flexible and secure auction architecture using trusted hardware. In: Proceedings of the International Workshop on Internet Computing and E-Commerce (ICEC) (2001) (Referenced on page 55.)

[156] Perrig, A., Song, D.: Hash visualization: A new technique to improve real-world security. In: Proceedings of the International Workshop on Cryptographic Techniques and E-Commerce (CrypTEC) (1999) (Referenced on page 71.)

[157] Pirker, M., Toegl, R., Hein, D., Danner, P.: A PrivacyCA for anonymity and trust. In: Proceedings of the International Conference on Trusted Computing (2009) (Referenced on page 23.)

[158] Pirker, M., Winkler, T., Toegl, R., Gissing, M.: IAIK jTpmTools - TPM tools for the Java platform. Source code v0.6: http://trustedjava.sourceforge.net/ (Referenced on page 59.)

[159] Ramachandran, A., Bhandankar, K., Tariq, M.B., Feamster, N.: Packets with provenance. Tech. Rep. GT-CS-08-02, Georgia Tech (2008) (Referenced on page 55.)

[160] Rudolph, C.: Covert identity information in direct anonymous attestation (DAA). In: Proceedings of the IFIP Information Security Conference (2007) (Referenced on page 24.)

[161] Sadeghi, A.R., Selhorst, M., Stüble, C., Wachsmann, C., Winandy, M.: TCG inside? - A note on TPM specification compliance. In: Proceedings of the ACM Workshop on Scalable Trusted Computing (STC) (2006) (Referenced on pages 51 and 68.)

[162] Sadeghi, A.R., Stueble, C.: Property-based attestation for computing platforms: caring about properties, not mechanisms. In: Proceedings of the Workshop on New Security Paradigms (NSPW) (2004) (Referenced on pages 32 and 33.)

[163] Sailer, R., Valdez, E., Jaeger, T., Perez, R., van Doorn, L., Griffin, J.L., Berger, S.: sHype: Secure hypervisor approach to trusted virtualized systems. Tech. Rep. RC23511, IBM Research (2005) (Referenced on page 27.)

[164] Sailer, R., Zhang, X., Jaeger, T., van Doorn, L.: Design and implementation of a TCG-based integrity measurement architecture. In: Proceedings of the USENIX Security Symposium (2004). Source code: http://linux-ima.sourceforge.net (Referenced on pages 6, 8, 9, 21, 22, 26, 41, 59, and 66.)

[165] Sarmenta, L., van Dijk, M., O'Donnell, C., Rhodes, J., Devadas, S.: Virtual monotonic counters and count-limited objects using a TPM without a trusted OS. In: Proceedings of the ACM Workshop on Scalable Trusted Computing (STC) (2006) (Referenced on page 56.)

[166] Saroiu, S., Wolman, A.: I am a sensor, and I approve this message. In: Proceedings of the ACM Workshop on Mobile Computing Systems and Applications (HotMobile) (2010) (Referenced on page 57.)

[167] Saxena, N., Ekberg, J.E., Kostiainen, K., Asokan, N.: Secure device pairing based on a visual channel (short paper). In: Proceedings of the IEEE Symposium on Security and Privacy (2006) (Referenced on page 71.)

[168] Schellekens, D., Tuyls, P., Preneel, B.: Embedded trusted computing with authenticated non-volatile memory. In: Proceedings of the International Conference on Trusted Computing (2008) (Referenced on page 39.)

[169] Schiffman, J., Moyer, T., Shal, C., Jaeger, T., McDaniel, P.: Justifying integrity using a virtual machine verifier. In: Proceedings of the Annual Computer Security Applications Conference (ACSAC) (2009) (Referenced on page 27.)

[170] Schneier, B., Kelsey, J.: Cryptographic support for secure logs on untrusted machines. In: Proceedings of the USENIX Security Symposium (1998) (Referenced on page 6.)

[171] Schwartz, E.J., Brumley, D., McCune, J.M.: A contractual anonymity system. In: Proceedings of the ISOC Symposium on Network and Distributed Systems Security (NDSS) (2010) (Referenced on page 56.)

[172] Seshadri, A., Luk, M., Qu, N., Perrig, A.: SecVisor: A tiny hypervisor to provide lifetime kernel code integrity for commodity OSes. In: Proceedings of the ACM Symposium on Operating Systems Principles (SOSP) (2007) (Referenced on page 32.)

[173] Seshadri, A., Luk, M., Shi, E., Perrig, A., van Doorn, L., Khosla, P.: Pioneer: Verifying integrity and guaranteeing execution of code on legacy platforms. In: Proceedings of ACM Symposium on Operating Systems Principles (SOSP) (2005) (Referenced on pages 39 and 40.)

[174] Seshadri, A., Perrig, A., van Doorn, L., Khosla, P.: SWATT: Software-based attestation for embedded devices. In: Proceedings of the IEEE Symposium on Security and Privacy (2004) (Referenced on pages 39 and 40.)

[175] Shaneck, M., Mahadevan, K., Kher, V., Kim, Y.: Remote software-based attestation for wireless sensors. In: Proceedings of European Workshop on Security and Privacy in Ad Hoc and Sensor Networks (ESAS) (2005) (Referenced on pages 39 and 40.)

[176] Shankar, U., Jaeger, T., Sailer, R.: Toward automated information-flow integrity verification for security-critical applications. In: Proceedings of the ISOC Symposium on Network and Distributed System Security (NDSS) (2006) (Referenced on pages 26 and 27.)

[177] Shi, E., Perrig, A., van Doorn, L.: BIND: A time-of-use attestation service for secure distributed systems. In: Proceedings of the IEEE Symposium on Security and Privacy (2005) (Referenced on pages 30 and 55.)

[178] Shubina, A., Bratus, S., Ingersol, W., Smith, S.W.: The diversity of TPMs and its effects on development: A case study of integrating the TPM into OpenSolaris. In: Proceedings of the ACM Workshop on Scalable Trusted Computing (STC) (2010) (Referenced on page 51.)

[179] Singaravelu, L., Pu, C., Haertig, H., Helmuth, C.: Reducing TCB complexity for security-sensitive applications: Three case studies. In: Proceedings of the ACM European Conference in Computer Systems (EuroSys) (2006) (Referenced on page 27.)

[180] Smith, S., Austel, V.: Trusting trusted hardware: Towards a formal model for programmable secure coprocessors. In: Proceedings of the USENIX Workshop on Electronic Commerce (1998) (Referenced on page 51.)

[181] Smith, S.W.: WebALPS: Using trusted co-servers to enhance privacy and security of web transactions. IBM Research Report RC-21851 (2000) (Referenced on page 55.)

[182] Smith, S.W.: Outbound authentication for programmable secure coprocessors. Journal of Information Security 3 (2004) (Referenced on pages 4, 19, 20, and 51.)

[183] Smith, S.W.: Trusted Computing Platforms: Design and Applications. Springer (2005) (Referenced on page 75.)

[184] Smith, S.W., Perez, R., Weingart, S.H., Austel, V.: Validating a high-performance, programmable secure coprocessor. In: Proceedings of the National Information Systems Security Conference (1999) (Referenced on pages 4, 14, 35, and 51.)

[185] Smith, S.W., Weingart, S.: Building a high-performance, programmable secure coprocessor. Computer Networks 31(8) (1999) (Referenced on pages 4, 14, 35, and 41.)

[186] Sophos: Best Buy digital photo frames ship with computer virus. http://www.sophos.com/pressoffice/news/articles/2008/01/photo-frame.html (2008) (Referenced on page 47.)

[187] Soriente, C., Tsudik, G., Uzun, E.: HAPADEP: Human-assisted pure audio device pairing. In: Proceedings of the International Information Security Conference (ISC) (2008) (Referenced on page 71.)

[188] Soriente, C., Tsudik, G., Uzun, E.: Secure pairing of interface constrained devices. International Journal on Security and Networks **4**(1) (2009) (Referenced on page 71.)

[189] Sparks, E.R.: A security assessment of trusted platform modules. Tech. Rep. TR2007-597, Dartmouth College (2007) (Referenced on page 21.)

[190] Spinellis, D.: Reflection as a mechanism for software integrity verification. ACM Transactions on Information and System Security **3**(1) (2000) (Referenced on pages 39 and 40.)

[191] Srivastava, A., Giffin, J.: Efficient monitoring of untrusted kernel-mode execution. In: Proceedings of the ISOC Symposium on Network and Distributed System Security (NDSS) (2011) (Referenced on page 32.)

[192] St. Clair, L., Schiffman, J., T., J., P, M.: Establishing and sustaining system integrity via root of trust installation. In: Proceedings of the Annual Computer Security Applications Conference (ACSAC) (2007) (Referenced on page 27.)

[193] Stajano, F., Anderson, R.: The resurrecting duckling: Security issues for ad-hoc wireless networks. In: Proceedings of the Security Protocols Workshop (1999) (Referenced on page 71.)

[194] STC '06: Proceedings of the ACM Workshop on Scalable Trusted Computing. ACM, New York, NY, USA (2006). 459065 (Referenced on page 76.)

[195] STC '07: Proceedings of the ACM Workshop on Scalable Trusted Computing. ACM, New York, NY, USA (2007). 537073 (Referenced on page 76.)

[196] STC '08: Proceedings of the ACM Workshop on Scalable Trusted Computing. ACM, New York, NY, USA (2008). 537081 (Referenced on page 76.)

[197] STC '09: Proceedings of the ACM Workshop on Scalable Trusted Computing. ACM, New York, NY, USA (2009). 459095 (Referenced on page 76.)

[198] STC '10: Proceedings of the ACM Workshop on Scalable Trusted Computing. ACM, New York, NY, USA (2010). 459105 (Referenced on page 76.)

[199] Strasser, M., Stamer, H., Molina, J.: Software-based TPM emulator. Source code: http://tpm-emulator.berlios.de/ (Referenced on page 59.)

[200] Stumpf, F., Tafreschi, O., Röder, P., Eckert, C.: A robust integrity reporting protocol for remote attestation. In: Proceedings of the Workshop on Advances in Trusted Computing (WATC) (2006) (Referenced on page 65.)

[201] Suh, G.E., Clarke, D., Gassend, B., van Dijk, M., Devadas, S.: AEGIS: Architecture for tamper-evident and tamper-resistant processing. In: Proceedings of the International Conference on Supercomputing (2003) (Referenced on pages 13 and 36.)

[202] Ta-Min, R., Litty, L., Lie, D.: Splitting interfaces: Making trust between applications and operating systems configurable. In: Proceedings of the USENIX Symposium on Operating Systems Design and Implementation (OSDI) (2006) (Referenced on page 27.)

[203] Tarnovsky, C.: Security failures in secure devices. In: Black Hat DC Presentation (2008) (Referenced on page 74.)

[204] Tip, F.: A survey of program slicing techniques. Journal of Programming Languages **3**(3), 121–189 (1995) (Referenced on page 31.)

[205] Toegl, R., Winkler, T., Steurer, M.E., Pirker, M., Pointner, C., Holzmann, T., Gissing, M., Sabongui, J.: IAIK jTSS - TCG software stack for the Java platform. Source code v0.6 `http://trustedjava.sourceforge.net/` (Referenced on page 59.)

[206] TrouSerS: The open-source TCG software stack. Source code: `http://trousers.sourceforge.net/` (Referenced on page 59.)

[207] Trusted Computing - Challenges and Applications, *Lecture Notes in Computer Science*, vol. 4968. Springer-Verlag, Berlin Germany (2008) (Referenced on page 76.)

[208] Trusted Computing, *Lecture Notes in Computer Science*, vol. 5471. Springer-Verlag, Berlin Germany (2009) (Referenced on page 76.)

[209] Trust and Trustworthy Computing, *Lecture Notes in Computer Science*, vol. 6101. Springer-Verlag, Berlin Germany (2010) (Referenced on page 76.)

[210] Trust and Trustworthy Computing, *Lecture Notes in Computer Science*, vol. 6740. Springer-Verlag, Berlin Germany (2011) (Referenced on page 76.)

[211] Trusted Computing Group: TCG mobile trusted module specification. Version 1.0, Revision 7.02 (2010) (Referenced on page 37.)

[212] Trusted Computing Group: PC client specific TPM interface specification (TIS). Version 1.21, Revision 1.00 (2011) (Referenced on page 31.)

[213] Trusted Computing Group: Trusted Platform Module Main Specification. Version 1.2, Revision 116 (2011) (Referenced on pages 4, 8, 15, 19, 20, 22, 23, 41, 66, and 67.)

[214] Türpe, S., Poller, A., Steffan, J., Stotz, J.P., Trukenmüller, J.: Attacking the BitLocker boot process. In: Proceedings of the International Conference on Trusted Computing (2009) (Referenced on page 53.)

[215] Vasudevan, A., Parno, B., Qu, N., Gligor, V.D., Perrig, A.: Lockdown: A safe and practical environment for security applications. Tech. Rep. CMU-CyLab-09-011, Carnegie Mellon University, Cylab (2009) (Referenced on pages 41, 42, and 70.)

[216] Vaudenay, S.: Secure communications over insecure channels based on short authenticated strings. In: Proceedings of CRYPTO (2005) (Referenced on page 71.)

[217] Vejda, T., Toegl, R., Pirker, M., Winkler, T.: Towards trust services for language-based virtual machines for grid computing. In: Proceedings of the International Conference on Trusted Computing (2008) (Referenced on page 10.)

[218] Wallace, C.: Worldwide PC market to double by 2010. Forrester Research, Inc. Press Release (2004) (Referenced on page 1.)

[219] Wave Systems Corp: Trusted Computing: An already deployed, cost effective, ISO standard, highly secure solution for improving Cybersecurity. `http://www.nist.gov/itl/upload/Wave-Systems_Cybersecurity-NOI-Comments_9-13-10.pdf` (2010) (Referenced on page 1.)

[220] Weigold, T., Kramp, T., Hermann, R., Höring, F., Buhler, P., Baentsch, M.:
The Zurich trusted information channel: An efficient defence against man-in-
the-middle and malicious software attacks. In: Proceedings of the International Conference on Trusted Computing (2008) (Referenced on page 69.)

[221] Weingart, S.: Physical security for the μABYSS system. In: Proceedings of
the IEEE Symposium on Security and Privacy (1987) (Referenced on page
36.)

[222] Weiser, M.: Program slicing. IEEE Transactions on Software Engineering
10(4), 352–357 (1984) (Referenced on page 31.)

[223] White, S., Weingart, S., Arnold, W., Palmer, E.: Introduction to the Citadel
architecture: Security in physically exposed environments. Tech. Rep.
RC16672, IBM T. J. Watson Research Center (1991) (Referenced on page
36.)

[224] Winter, J.: Trusted computing building blocks for embedded Linux-based
ARM Trustzone platforms. In: Proceedings of the ACM Workshop on Scalable Trusted Computing (STC) (2008) (Referenced on page 38.)

[225] Wurster, G., van Oorschot, P., Somayaji, A.: A generic attack on
checksumming-based software tamper resistance. In: Proceedings of the
IEEE Symposium on Security and Privacy (2005) (Referenced on page 40.)

[226] Yee, B.S.: Using secure coprocessors. Ph.D. thesis, Carnegie Mellon University (1994) (Referenced on page 36.)

[227] Zhuang, X., Zhang, T., Lee, H., Pande, S.: Hardware assisted control flow
obfuscation for embedded processors. In: Proceedings of the Conference on
Compilers, Architecture and Synthesis for Embedded Systems (2004) (Referenced on page 38.)

Index